Y0-CYQ-503

The Piano

Keynote Books

By Bill Ballantine: THE VIOLIN
THE FLUTE
THE PIANO

Forthcoming Titles:

THE CLARINET

THE GUITAR

THE TRUMPET

DRUMS AND OTHER PERCUSSION INSTRUMENTS

THE CELLO

THE SAXOPHONE

THE TROMBONE

THE HORNS

THE OBOE

THE VIOLA

Rudolf Serkin.

A KEYNOTE BOOK

The Piano

An Introduction to the Instrument

by Bill Ballantine

Franklin Watts, Inc.
845 Third Avenue
New York, N.Y. 10022

Photographs courtesy of:

RCA Records, pages 10, 26, 73, 75, 77, 79, and 80.
Columbia Records, frontispiece and page 94.
Steinway & Sons, pages 15, 19, 21, 56, and 60.
Metropolitan Museum of Art, The Crosby Brown Collection of Musical Instruments, 1889, pages 35, 38, 42, and 48.
Smithsonian Institution, pages 44, 45, 46, 48, 50, 51, 52, and 53.
Library of Congress, pages 70, 73, 83, 89, 91, and 93.
Columbia Broadcasting System, pages 77 and 80.

SBN 531-01843-1
Library of Congress Catalog Card Number: 79-114926
© Copyright 1971 by Franklin Watts, Inc.
Printed in the United States of America

Contents

The Piano

Vladimir Horowitz.

Prelude

The favorite musical instrument of home and concert seems to be the piano. More than 21 million people in the United States play it—about two-thirds as many as the 32 million people who play all the other musical instruments combined.

There are advantages in the piano as an instrument. You can make music on it right from the start. There is no fumbling for notes as on the fingerboard of a violin or other stringed instruments. There is no learning to make notes with your lips and with valves as there is on the horns. On a piano, the notes are all laid out before the player, in eighty-eight black and white keys. Touch a key, and there is a musical note—always the note that correctly matches that particular key. And the same note sounds each time that key is pressed. The music is always there.

A beginning violinist must work hard before he can play even the simplest piece in tune and with an attractive tone. But a pianist, in his first introduction to the keyboard, can produce an agreeable one-finger melody. Sometimes he may hit the wrong notes, but he cannot play too flat or too sharp unless the piano itself is off pitch. The player's ear has no part in deciding a piano's tone: it is ready-made.

The piano's highest note and its lowest can be struck at once, since the length of the keyboard is just a comfortable arm span. In less than two seconds, the keys of a piano can be played in rapid succession by running a finger or thumb from one end of the keyboard to the other. Foot pedals make notes soft or loud.

This book is not one of instruction on how to play. Rather, it tells about the instrument itself: what it is and how its sound is made; where it came from and who its early inventors and makers were. The intricacies of present-day piano manufacture are explained. Some piano composers and a few notable concert pianists and jazz performers are introduced. There are suggestions for taking care of your piano.

Perhaps, because this book will help you to know more about the piano, you will gain a deeper understanding and appreciation of the instrument and its music. And perhaps you will enjoy piano concerts more because of it. For those wishing to go deeper into piano lore, there are lists of suggested books for further reading and reference. A list of recordings of piano music is included, because a good way to learn about the instrument is to listen to others playing it well.

1.   The Piano, Its Sound and Action

The piano is a stringed musical instrument played by the hands striking a keyboard.

The word "piano" is short for *pianoforte*, an Italian word meaning "soft" (*piano*) and "strong" (*forte*) together. The name was given the early piano because it could produce both soft tones and strong (that is, loud) ones—something that could not be done by the keyboard instruments that came before it.

Among musical instruments the piano is unsurpassed in range of pitch (height and depth of tone), dynamics (loudness and softness), and polyphony (combination of individual but harmonizing melodies). The piano can play ten notes at once; most musical instruments, including the human voice, can manage only one at a time. The piano is most expressive; its notes reach from full deep bass to thin delicate soprano. All sorts of wonderful effects can be achieved with its rich sound. On a piano, both melody and accompaniment can be played together. In works prepared for four hands, a piano produces enough music to keep two performers busy on one keyboard.

Yet the piano does not have to be the star. It can cooperate beautifully with strings and woodwinds, and can provide musical background for the melodies of soloists.

One of the piano's drawbacks is that it cannot hold a long

note, as wind instruments or stringed instruments can. As soon as a piano note is played, it begins to fade. It cannot be made progressively louder. This is because once the note is struck, no new sound is being created, as it is when a horn is blown or a violin bowed. The piano, therefore, can never equal the human voice, a wind instrument, or a stringed instrument in producing a truly unbroken "singing" flow of tone.

Such a failing does not hurt the piano's popularity among beginners. In America there are six times as many piano students as there are students of the violin. So, more music is prepared for the piano than for strings, and the learner has a great variety of piano pieces to choose from.

A pianist has another advantage in that he does not have to carry his instrument with him when he is going to perform. There will be a piano waiting: at home or with friends; at school; in church; at auditoriums; in dance halls and concert halls. The professional concert artist selects his piano from a dealer and it is brought to the place where he will play it. And the player does not have to tune his piano. That exacting job is done by a professional tuner.

Pianos have two principal shapes: grand and upright. The sound-producing mechanisms of both are concealed within cases of handsomely finished wood; only the keyboards are exposed.

The grand is the oldest type of piano. Roughly triangular, or harp-shaped, it is mounted in a lying-down position on three legs, as a table, with the strings running horizontally away from the keyboard. Grand pianos range from massive concert grands down to standard grands and baby grands.

The upright piano is a rectangular box, standing erect on one of its longer narrow sides, with the strings set vertically behind the keyboard. Uprights are large, medium, and small

Above, a modern grand piano and, below, a modern upright.

—or standard, spinet, and studio. The studio piano is compact enough to tuck into the smallest modern apartment. The portable upright is even smaller. And there is one piano that folds into suitcase size. It is used mostly by conductors, orchestrators, composers, and concert soloists as a practice instrument while on tour.

For an understanding of how the piano makes its sound, it is first necessary to realize that any sound—all sound—is the result of a reaction of the auditory nerves in the ears to vibrations carried in air and water. This reaction is what we call hearing.

When force is applied against an object—when it is struck, for instance—it moves rapidly back and forth in space. Sometimes the movement is so slight as to be invisible. This movement is called vibration. An object's movement, or vibration, causes the air around it to be disturbed. The disturbances go out in all directions from the vibrating object, in regular patterns called sound waves. When a pebble is dropped into a pool, circular waves spread from the point where the stone has struck. With sound waves, however, the ripples radiate in all directions and not just in circles on a flat surface. And, of course, sound waves themselves are invisible. When they reach our ears, we hear.

To see the vibrations that cause sound waves, extend the handle of a silver dinner knife out from the edge of a table. Anchor the knife there by bearing down with one hand on the tip of the blade. Then pluck the handle sharply with your other hand. The knife will shake up and down and make a humming sound.

You can feel sound by lightly touching your fingers to your throat as you speak or by placing them on top of an operating television set, radio, or record player.

The piano is a stringed percussion instrument. (The word

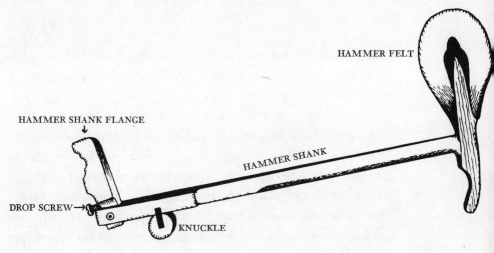

HAMMER FELT

HAMMER SHANK FLANGE

HAMMER SHANK

DROP SCREW →

KNUCKLE

A *piano hammer*.

"percussion" comes from a Latin word meaning "beaten" or "struck.") The piano's sound waves come from strings that vibrate when they are struck by small felt-headed hammers. The hammers are operated by a player's fingers when he pushes down the piano's keys.

The hammers strike steel-wire strings mounted on a harp-shaped metal frame enclosed in the piano's case. A vibrating piano string by itself is a poor sender of sound. It needs help. That is why piano strings are strung over a low wooden bridge glued to a soundboard. The bridge vibrates when the strings are struck, and it causes the soundboard to vibrate as well. Because more objects are now vibrating, more sound waves are made.

Such reinforcement of the original sound by the vibration of another object or other objects is called resonance. To see how this works, pinch with your fingers and quickly release the prongs of a silver fork. The vibrating prongs will make a soft *hum-m-m*. Now pinch and release them again, but this time touch the end of the fork's handle to a wooden table-top. At the touch, the humming sound will become much louder, because the vibrating fork has made the tabletop vibrate. Since it has more area than the fork, the tabletop gives off more vibrations and sets more air in motion, so making more sound.

The highness or lowness of a tone is called its pitch. Fast vibrations (high frequency) make a tone of high pitch. Slow vibrations (low frequency) make a tone of low pitch. In stringed instruments such as the piano, the thickness of a string, its length, and its tension affect the pitch. Heavy (thick) strings vibrate more slowly; lightweight (thin) ones are fast vibrators. Slack strings vibrate more slowly than taut ones. The longer a string is, the slower its vibrations, and therefore the lower its pitch. Short strings vibrate faster and have higher pitch. As proof, try this. Stretch a rubber band between two fixed points and twang it. Note the tone. Now pinch off the band with your finger at some point beyond its middle. Twang the rubber again. This time the tone will be higher because, by pinching the band, you have shortened its vibrating length.

A piano can play higher than a piccolo and lower than a double bass. The tonal range of a piano with a normal-sized keyboard is seven and one-quarter octaves. An octave is the succession of eight tones that make up our usual musical scale. An eight-tone scale, called a diatonic scale, is played by striking the piano's white keys. In each octave of the piano, five black keys fill in. When all the keys, black and white, are played in progression, they make what is called a chromatic scale—a scale of twelve notes, with the black keys sounding just half a tone-step between the white keys on either side.

To find out how the piano's many tones get their different pitches, lift the lid and look inside your piano. You will see from 240 to 253 strings stretched on a cast-iron frame, roughly triangular. Note that some keys have more than one string.

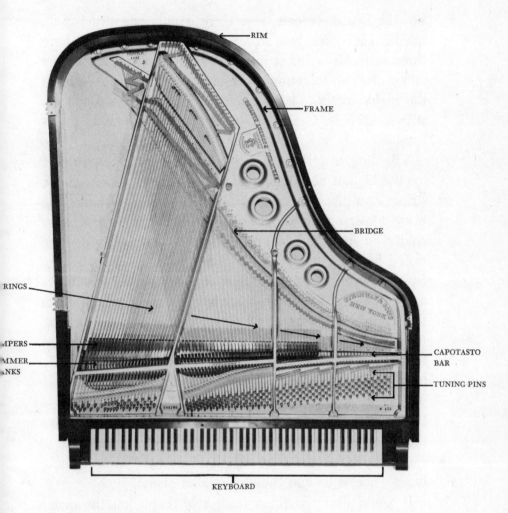

RIM

FRAME

BRIDGE

RINGS

MPERS

MMER
NKS

CAPOTASTO
BAR

TUNING PINS

KEYBOARD

A modern grand piano: interior view from the top.

For the lowest, or bass, keys there is only one string each; middle keys have two strings each; and upper keys have three each. Since the strings for the upper keys are thinner and set less air vibrating, three are needed to get volume in the higher notes. The pairs and triplets are called unison strings; each of a group is struck at the same time by its hammer.

Vibrating lengths of strings vary from about two inches for the highest note to several feet for the lowest. If all the strings of a piano had the same tightness and thickness, the piano's lowest note would need a string 20 to 30 feet long. And even so, in strings of such length, the quality of tone would be poor unless very large hammers did the striking. By the use of thicker and looser strings, however, low notes can be produced without depending on string length alone. Bass strings are wrapped in heavy copper wire to increase their thickness, to slow down vibrations, and so to make up for the shortness of these strings—a shortness made necessary by the limited space inside the piano's cabinet. In most pianos, to make bass strings longer, they are overstrung— that is, they are carried diagonally across the frame above the other strings. One reason for the superior sound of a concert grand is the extra length of its bass strings—sometimes twice as long as those of smaller pianos.

A piano string stretches from a hitch pin on the metal frame's sweep-curve side to a tuning pin on the other side, nearest the keyboard. The tuning pins are tightly fitted into a heavy wooden board called the wrest plank, or pin block, which is behind the keyboard. A string's useful vibrating length lies between the bridge and the *capotasto* bar—also popularly known as the *captasto*, or cappydaster—which is made of heavy metal and is a solidly fixed part of the frame. This bar bridges the strings just before they tie off at the

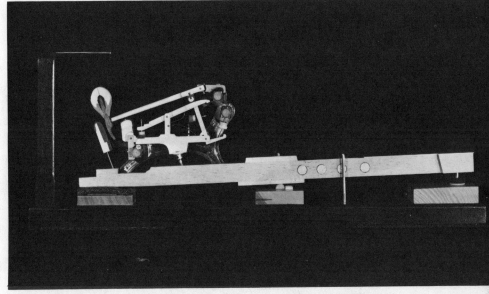

The action of a grand piano; from a model made by Steinway & Sons.

tuning pins. It keeps the strings in place much as the finger-board nut does on a violin. The hammers strike the strings just in front of the *capotasto* bar.

A piano's "action" is the operation of its keys and its hammers against its strings. The action is a complex, delicately balanced mechanical affair involving many sensitive levers. When a piano key is pressed down, that force is sent by beautifully timed precision movements to the hammer. From its normal position about two inches away from its string or strings the hammer flies up to strike them at about the same speed with which the finger hit the key. At the same time, a felt-capped strip of wood called a damper is automatically lifted from the string to allow it to vibrate. As soon as the finger leaves the key, the damper drops back onto the string to stop its vibration. To get a maximum effect, the hammer must fly toward the string with some speed and be able to rebound instantly—a hit-and-run blow so swift that the string's vibrations are not deadened.

A device known as double escapement, patented in 1821, allows the hammer after its rebound to repeat its action before the key has returned to its original level. In other words, the same note can be quickly replayed—again and again.

The struck vibrating string of a piano produces not just one tone, but many. The strongest and loudest is the fundamental tone of the string. The number of its vibrations is the tone's pitch. The other tones, of lower intensity, are called overtones or harmonics—faint sounds that enrich the sound of the fundamental tone. Overtones are always present, but are heard more when the piano key is struck hard, for then the vibration lasts longer and there is more breakdown of partial vibrations. The individual tone quality of a piano depends on the particular overtones it has and how strong they are.

A piano's foot pedals, when used with sensitive judgment by a skillful pianist, can add marvelous color to the instrument's tones. The pedal to the pianist's right is the most important. Commonly called the loud pedal, it is also known as the damper pedal. Perhaps more accurately, it is an "undamper" pedal. When stepped on, it raises all the dampers from every string at once, no matter which notes are being played. With the dampers up, all the notes struck keep on sounding and setting up sympathetic vibrations in the strings not being played, so adding volume throughout the instrument. Wisely used, the "un-damper" pedal lets the player go smoothly from one note to another, by permitting the first note to continue to sound after the finger has left its key and gone on to the next note.

The pedal on the left is the soft pedal. It makes tones softer by one of three methods. It may either bring a strip of felt between the hammers and the strings, or it may bring the hammers nearer the strings so that their blows are not so strong. If you have done carpentry, you know that a big hammer swing has more force than one made from a point close to the object being hit. The best soft-pedal method of all, favored in the finest modern pianos, shifts the hammers when high notes are played, so that only two of the three strings provided for them are struck. During this shift action, the dampers react as usual, rising from all three strings as soon as the key is pressed down. As a result, the vibrations of the two struck strings cause sympathetic vibrations in the third, or unstruck, string. These vibrations made without the hammer's blow, while not loud, are enough to add color to the tone. Such sympathetic vibrations greatly benefit soft passages in the high notes.

Not all pianos have a middle pedal. And it is not there, as Victor Borge, the pianist comedian, contends, to keep the other pedals apart. Ordinarily the middle pedal is called the *sostenuto*, or "sustaining," pedal; it was invented in 1862 in France and was known at first as a *pédale de prolongement*, a "pedal of prolongation." When it is stepped on, it catches and holds up the dampers of only those notes being played at that moment. A chord can be kept going while the hand that made it goes on to other notes that will stop sounding as soon as their keys return to their original normal level. On certain pianos the middle pedal is not a true *sostenuto*, but serves only as a lift for bass-section dampers.

Today's piano is ingeniously constructed to make the most of the notes that are sounded, but much depends on the person who plays it.

2. Your Piano and You

It is fun to play a piano. You can even learn by yourself to do it. There are books that will help with the fundamentals. You can teach yourself to play by ear or by reading music, which is the best way by far. Many pianists are self-taught. But the finest have had good teachers.

The piano is exciting; it has more power than any other solo instrument. And while power is not the most desirable musical quality, to be in control of a piano is certainly satisfying.

Some of the pleasure of piano playing comes from the direct physical challenge—the rhythmic use of one's muscles. And sometimes, banging a few chords on a piano is a great relief for emotions that have been held in.

Because it is a percussion instrument, the piano speaks its rhythms crisply and with certainty. It can have the same kind of primitive wildness that a drum has. It is not, however, just an instrument for drumming. Think of it as a miniature orchestra. It can make sounds as delicate as a mouse's whisper or as bold as the rolls and crashes of thunder.

Most great pianists agree that the age of a beginning piano student does not matter; even adults can be learners. Josef Hofmann, a great concert pianist, once said, "Age need not stand in your way, provided there is gift and intelligence." But no one will be a good pianist if piano music does not thrill him deep inside and make him want to play it himself. That is essential. And besides a burning desire to play, there must be a down-to-earth will to work and an ability to concentrate, as well as a great deal of patience, self-discipline, and self-reliance. It is mostly up to any beginner whether he will be a pianist or merely a key-pounder.

To gain skill at the piano, a person should try to achieve a nice balance between spending too much of himself at it and becoming exhausted, and sparing himself too much. No task is too difficult when the right tempo is found. When asked if a particularly exacting role was hard, a famous actor once said, "Nothing you can *do* is hard to do." And so it is with piano playing. A Mendelssohn song, a Beethoven concerto, a Brahms sonata—easy, if you can *do* it.

While you may not need a perfect ear for tone in order to play a piano, a few things must be developed if your music is to be something more than tiresome pounding. To bring piano music fully to life, you will need a sensitive touch. This does not mean that you must lovingly caress the keys or make great showy swoops and flourishes with your arms. On the contrary, "touch" means the determination and speed with which a pianist strikes a key. That is the only way he can control individual tones, because such decisive action regulates the striking speed of the hammers. If a piano key is touched very gently, no tone at all will result. The art of piano playing lies in the player's skill at striking keys at varying speeds and intervals, and working the pedals so that some tones will be slightly louder or softer than others and there will be variations in the lapses of time between tones.

You will also need a feeling for tempo—the rate of speed of music—and tone color, or timbre. Tone color is the quality of a tone: thick, thin, light, dark, sharp, dull, smooth, rough, warm, cold, velvety, fuzzy, rounded, and so forth. Your play-

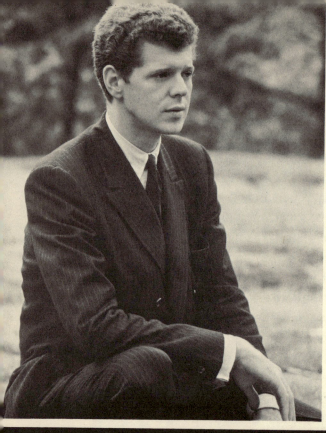

Pianists,
young and old:
Van Cliburn (left)
and Artur Schnabel
(below).

ing will be flat and uninteresting until you learn to weave color into your tones by taking full advantage of the piano's built-in *pianoforte*—its capacity for contrasting strongness and softness.

You will have to develop fingering technique. In playing a piano, both hands and all fingers are used at the same time, and often both hands must play many notes at the same instant. Stringed instruments use only one hand for fingering; with wind instruments, only one note at a time is played— ever so much simpler. In piano, a difficult thing is training the fingers to play evenly, as they are of different strengths. With practice, this becomes automatic.

The best way to learn fingering technique is from a good book of finger exercises. Your teacher will know which one is best for you at each stage of your development. Practice the exercises regularly. Isidor Philipp's *Exercises for Independence of the Fingers, Part I*, is very useful to amateur pianists. It is available at most music stores. When you become more skilled, look into the little-known technical exercises written by Johannes Brahms—*Brahms' 51 Uebungen*. You will find them and many others described in a fascinating book by Charles Cooke: *Playing the Piano for Pleasure*.

Ideally, the hand of a pianist has broad palms, spoon- or spatula-shaped fingers—with the little one almost as long as the middle one—and a very wide stretch. Actually, pianists' hands vary tremendously. For example, Josef Hofmann had such a small hand that he could not strike an octave. Van Cliburn can strike a span over ten notes with ease. Many pianists have stubby fingers, which are often stronger than long ones. The important thing is that they have ample spread, so that the hands will have as wide a stretch as possible.

To make the fingers stronger and more limber, close them

Daniel Barenboim practicing at home.

so that their tops rest on the fleshy cushions at their bases. Now slowly extend each finger, one at a time, while keeping the others clenched shut. Repeat until your fingers are tired. As you use your hands more and more on the piano keyboard they will loosen up and your stretch will increase.

One of the advantages of the piano is that it is played sitting down. Do not crowd up against the keyboard, and do not sit so far back that you must stretch your arms to reach it. Be comfortable when you face the keys.

Stiffness is a common fault among amateur pianists. Do not be tense at the keyboard; feel relaxed, and heavy from the shoulders to the fingertips. Particularly, loosen the arms and hands. Dangle your arms at your sides, then, still relaxed, lift your hands to the keyboard.

Some professionals like to be stiff while practicing. Percy Grainger, the Australian virtuoso, worked opposing muscles against each other to develop strength. Sergei Rachmaninoff often spoke of stiffness. But playing the piano is not an athletic exercise; practice and play the way your body feels best. Do what is natural.

A piano with easy action is usually better for an amateur, for at first his playing is mostly with the muscles of his fingers and the weight of his hands. Professionals prefer the resistance of a piano with stiffer action, because in playing they use their arms, shoulders, and backs as well as their hands. You should learn to do this.

After you have become a good player, daily practice is not necessary. You can play the piano pretty well even after months away from it. But to become a good player in the first place requires a great deal of practice. Think of it positively. Do not look on it as a dull chore, but as a way to improve your playing.

At practice, learn to concentrate. Put everything out of your mind except your piano keys and their music. Sometimes, particularly when you are a beginner, it is a good idea to have someone stand by during lessons, to take notes as the teacher uncovers mistakes and weaknesses—then later to see that these are corrected at practice. Try not to repeat mistakes, and try not to learn things wrong. It takes much longer to unlearn something and relearn it another way than to learn it right at first. Be thorough. Slow practice makes for quick playing. Be hard on yourself. Judge every tone as though someone else were making it.

Quality of practice is better than *quantity*. One hour daily will work wonders. This practice hour can be divided into several parts and fitted in around other daily activities. Several short snatches of practice sometimes beat one long, tiresome stretch. Making up for missed practice time by adding it onto future sessions will not work. It is much better to be steady, and practice at the same time each day. Do not practice when you are tired.

To keep from being a clock watcher, get yourself an inexpensive timer, of the kind used in the kitchen to keep track of periods of cooking. Such a device will let you know when five minutes is up, or a half hour, or whatever time span you choose to set.

Do not play on an untuned piano. Piano tuning should be regular. Three tunings a year are about right, unless the piano is played a great deal. In that case, every six weeks is better.

Rely on your teacher's advice regarding the use of a metronome, a mechanical tempo-indicator that produces regular beats. Some pianists feel that depending on a metronome kills the natural musical pulse and harms true expression in playing. Very often, counting aloud or silently to yourself will mark time just as well.

It is important to have the ability to absorb whatever is taught you and to make it your own. Aim at reading music as easily as you would a newspaper or a book. Make it your goal to learn many different kinds of musical pieces, and not just classical concert numbers. Try to keep your musical outlook from becoming narrow.

Above all else, keep in mind that the piano requires from you a certain amount of temperament—a little fire. Approach it with a sense of joy. Learn to play the piano as though you were having a lively, interesting conversation with an old friend. The more you talk together, the more you will understand each other.

3. The Piano's History

The piano is of the chordophone, or "string sound," family. Its earliest ancestor is the musical bow, which made the very first musical note from a string. Such bows appear in Stone Age cave drawings dating back many thousands of years. The musical bow is a stick bent by the tension of a thong, which makes a musical tone when twanged.

Over many centuries, several families of stringed musical instruments branched from the musical bow: those of the harp, lyre, lute, and zither. From the harp line has come only that one present-day instrument, the harp. From the lyre and lute families have come the guitar, the banjo, and the violin and its cousins the viola, the cello, and the double bass. And the zither group produced the piano.

The piano's most remote recognizable relative is the ancient Greek monochord, or "one string," devised about 550 B.C. by Pythagoras, the Greek philosopher and mathematician. It consisted of a single gut or metal string, stretched between two bridges resting on a sound box. In order to demonstrate the fundamental laws of harmonics and to teach pitch, a third bridge was moved along under the taut string to any one of a number of points that had been mathematically figured out. In 2650 B.C., even before Pythagoras, the Chinese used an instrument called the ke, which was similar to the monochord.

By the end of the Middle Ages—which lasted until about 1450—or by about the beginning of the fifteenth century, the monochord had evolved into the polychord, "many strings." One large polychord had seventy strings—some in unison—which passed over five bridges and were struck by brass hammers. The polychord's tone was very soft.

After a keyboard was added to the polychord, it became known as the clavichord—from *clavis*, Latin for "key," and *chord*, for "string." Some musical historians claim that the clavichord existed as early as the twelfth century, but the oldest dated one was made in A.D. 1543. It is now in the musical instrument collection of Leipzig University, in Germany.

The earliest European mention of a stringed keyboard instrument was in A.D. 1323, in a book called *Musica Speculativa*. The first stringed instrument with a keyboard was probably the *clavicytherium*, or keyed cithara, descended from a Greek zither.

The keyboard itself originated with the Greeks in the second century A.D., on a water-pressure organ called a *hydraulos*.

The clavichord was played by tangent, or touch, action. Its strings were made to vibrate by being struck with small brass wedges, or tangents, set upright on the far ends of pivoted wooden levers operated by the keys. A wedge remained on a string until the finger left the key. The sound was sweet and delicate; even the loudest tones were very soft. The nature of the clavichord's action gave its player more intimate control than that afforded by any other keyboard instrument.

Usually a clavichord was small enough to be carried under the arm. Some were larger; a few had legs. The instrument was favored by ladies. Oddly, no music was written specifically for the clavichord for nearly two hundred years. The earliest

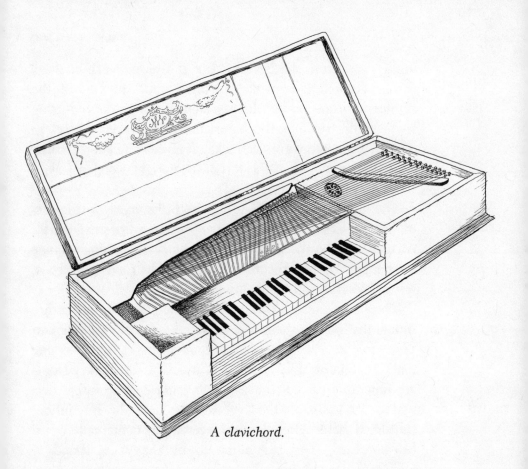

A clavichord.

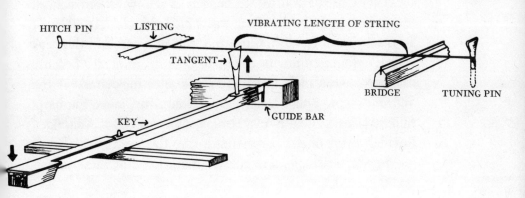

HITCH PIN   LISTING   VIBRATING LENGTH OF STRING

TANGENT→

BRIDGE   TUNING PIN

GUIDE BAR

KEY→

The action of the clavichord.

music dates from the beginning of the seventeenth century.

The clavichord remained in favor until the end of the eighteenth century, developing along with a *plucked*-string keyboard instrument, the harpsichord. Its strings are set in motion by a plectrum, or pick, of raven's quill or leather, carried on a tongue at the top of an upright wooden jack, a short stick.

The harpsichord is rich in high and dissonant, or disagreeing, harmonics, which to some people sound extremely harsh. At first hearing, the instrument's crisp sparkle seems strange —even jarring—but the tone is admirably robust, brilliant, warm, colorful, full, and round.

The harpsichord evolved from a mediaeval Greek zither called the psaltery (from *psallein*, Greek for "pulling" or "plucking"). The oldest harpsichord definitely dated is one made by Hieronymus of Bologna in A.D. 1521. Its key fronts are fancifully carved; the cabinet's surface is profusely decorated. In Latin on the keyboard cover is the inscription, translated here: "Behold how everything contained in air, heaven, earth, and sea is moved by the sweet sound of melody."

As early as the fourteenth century a primitive harpsichord was in use in Italy, where it was called the *clavicembalo*, or key psaltery, in English. One kind that hung around the neck was called an *istrumento di porco*, "pig instrument," because it looked like a pig's head. Germans later nicknamed it the *Schweinskopf*—"pig's head," in German. In France the harpsichord was called a *clavecin*; in Germany, a *Keilflügel*. Smaller forms of the harpsichord were the spinet, which was rectangular in shape, and the virginal. Some of these instruments were legless.

Bigger than the clavichord, the regular-sized harpsichord stood on legs and had the graceful wing shape of the modern

A harpsichord made in 1650; note the two keyboards.

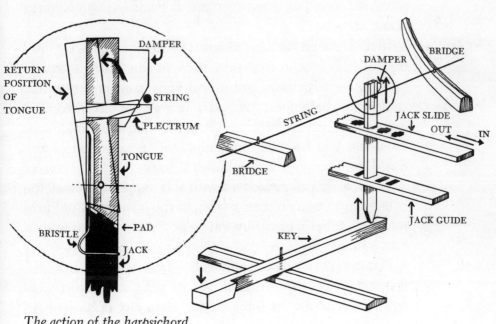

The action of the harpsichord.

grand piano; varying lengths of strings could be fitted into it.

The harpsichord ranged from a simple one-keyboard in-strument with one string for each key to elaborate later models with two keyboards and four or five strings for each key, controlled by hand stops and other tone-altering devices. A lute stop made a hard, powerful, bright tone. Harp, or buff, stops muffled the tone. Double keyboards brought out melody over accompaniment and permitted contrasts of tone by the use of quill picks on one keyboard—for cold tones—and leather ones on the other—for warm tones. With pedals, a player could throw the two keyboards together. The normal compass of the larger harpsichords was four octaves. Later, in Bach's time, the compass was extended to five.

Early in the eighteenth century there arose a demand for louder music than could be played by the clavichord or the harpsichord. Over the years various efforts were made to im-prove the sound of those instruments by adapting a hammer action to them.

In 1721, a previously unknown German musician, Chris-toph Gottlieb Schroeter, submitted to the King of Saxony his idea for a keyboard instrument with hammer action that could play both loud and soft. It was not accepted. But even earlier, as far back as 1709, the Italian Bartolommeo Cristofori had been experimenting with a new kind of key-board instrument, which he called a *gravicembalo col piano e forte*, or a "large harpsichord with soft and loud." Cristofori continued to turn out new models of the instrument until the mid 1720's, but the century was half over before his invention finally caught on.

Hammer action came to the piano from the dulcimer. The first record of this instrument is a carved-stone picture from 667 B.C., found at the site of Nineveh, a city of ancient Assyria. It shows a king viewing a parade. The dulcimer in the drawing hangs from its player's neck and is being struck by a stick held in his right hand, while the palm of the other hand lies on the strings to check the tone. Probably this is the earliest evidence of piano action—of strings being both hammered and muffled.

The modern piano has five of the important characteristics of the clavichord: an independent soundboard; a device that prevents vibrations of the strings not in use; a cloth to deaden vibration from the ends of strings beyond the bridge; groups of strings tuned in unison; and tone made from a blow, instead of by plucking. From the harpsichord the piano took these ideas: the shape of the grand; the sustaining pedal; the pedal felt for soft playing; the transposing keyboard; and the soft stop for quiet tones.

Thomas Jefferson had a piano sent over to Monticello from England in 1771. By 1774, pianos were being made in America by John Behrent. A few years later, Vienna boasted more than three hundred piano teachers.

As the century drew to a close, the piano was firmly established as a musical instrument. It then had a five-octave normal range and sixty-one keys—not eighty-eight, as it has today. Mostly, pedals were worked by the knees, but the foot pedal, introduced in England, was catching on. The framing still was wooden; the iron frame had not yet been thought of. The strings and hammers often broke. The tone and action were very light.

Until the early years of the nineteenth century, two types of piano appealed to professional pianists: the Viennese piano and the English piano. The action of the first was light, had little carrying power, and needed very little pressure on the keys. The tone was round and flutelike. The English

An early English spinet, made by Thomas Hitchcock about 1700.

An ornately decorated nineteenth-century piano.

piano was bigger, more heavily strung, more brilliant in sound, and more difficult to play, but better able to produce showy technical effects.

Compared to modern pianos, many of the earliest ones looked awkward. Most were like pieces of overwrought furniture—thick-legged and heavily carved. It seems unlikely that they could make delicate music. The designs were fancy and the outer-case decorations unbelievably elaborate. Some of the instruments were almost smothered by decoration—ivory and precious stones, silver and gold, colored glass and enamels. Many of the pianos had paintings and complicated inlay work inside their lids. The entire outside cases of some instruments were painted with fanciful designs in oils.

Because the strings of many of these pianos were mounted vertically above and behind the keyboard, the instruments looked tall and top-heavy. Some of these so-called pyramid pianos that were made in Prague even had clocks in their string towers. A similar skyscraper was a piano called the giraffe. The fanciest giraffes, with the most ornate carving, were made in Czechoslovakia. Another curious piano of those pioneer days was the pedal pianoforte, made about 1815. It consisted of a normal piano with a keyboard for fingering, and a second, legless instrument on which the first one stood. The keyboard of the lower piano was operated by the feet, like the pedals of an organ.

Some of these interesting old-time keyboard instruments are now owned by the art museums of large cities, and are on display. In New York City, the Metropolitan Museum of Art has the Crosby Brown collection of beautifully ornamented clavichords and harpsichords. There, one of Bartolommeo Cristofori's first *fortepianos*, made in Florence, Italy, in 1720, can be seen.

In Europe there are many museums devoted to musical

instruments. In London, there is the Benton Fletcher collection of early keyboard instruments, at Fenton House, in Hampstead. Also in London, at the Victoria and Albert Museum, is a lavishly decorated spinet made by Annibale dei Rossi of Milan. It is adorned with precious and semiprecious stones: turquoise, garnet, lapis lazuli, emerald, topaz, sapphire, amethyst, pearl, jasper, carnelian, and ruby. One of the virginals that belonged to Elizabeth I, Queen of England, is also there. Its cypress-wood case is covered with crimson Genoa velvet and lined with yellow tabby silk, a taffeta with wavy markings. The keys have gold, silver, and ivory inlay work.

Munich, West Germany, has the state musical-instrument collection. In Paris, there are collections in the Louvre Museum and the Instrumental Museum of the National Higher Conservatory of Music. There are many, many more—in Leipzig, Berlin, Amsterdam, Copenhagen, Stockholm, and Vienna.

A few interesting books about antique keyboard musical instruments are listed at the back of this book. Dip into them. The more you learn about the family background of your piano, the better you will be able to make it a part of your own family.

4. Famous Makers of Pianos

In 1698, in Florence, Italy, a harpsichord maker of Padua named Bartolommeo di Francesco Cristofori was employed by a rich and powerful prince named Ferdinando de Medici. Under orders from de Medici, Cristofori began to build keyboard musical instruments that would "speak like the heart, sometimes with the delicate touch of an angel, at others with a violent burst of passion." By 1700, Cristofori had made four of the instruments that he called arpicembalos, or harp dulcimers. In Ferdinando de Medici's listing, this instrument is described as a "new invention that plays piano and forte, with keys and some dampers of red cloth touching the strings and some hammers that make the piano and forte." Ferdinando liked it, but almost nobody else seemed to. The elegant ladies of the court found the arpicembalo too indelicate. The idea of hitting strings with hammers appealed only to the pot swabbers in the kitchens, the court jesters, and the children of the nobility. (Cristofori's hammer action was not the first ever known. There is a record of a similar device in Holland in 1610.)

But in 1709, Cristofori made a better instrument. Soon it was named the fortepiano. Still no one paid much attention to it—not even when, in 1711, a well-respected journalist, the Marchese Scipione Maffei, published a paper praising the fortepiano.

Early piano made by Cristofori in 1720.

There was no demand for it. Music lovers of the period were content with the old instruments. They were adequate for the intimate chamber concerts then in style; musicians felt no real need for anything louder. They cherished their tinkly clavichords and harpsichords, "lonely, melancholy, indescribably sweet instruments."

But in 1725 the Marchese Maffei's essay about Cristofori's invention was translated into German by König, the court poet at Dresden. He was a close friend of a renowned organ builder and clavichord and harpsichord maker, Gottfried Silbermann. Inspired by what he read, Silbermann built two *fortepianos*. Both were failures. Their trebles were too weak and the touch was too heavy. Silbermann took most of his ideas from the very simple conception of the *fortepiano* that had been given to the King of Saxony by the young German Schroeter. A model of it had trustingly been left at the court for consideration.

By 1726, Cristofori had perfected his instrument. It then had all the essentials of a modern piano: keys, double-action hammers against wire strings, dampers, and escapement. By that time, Cristofori is believed to have produced twenty instruments, two of which survive. His invention still was considered nothing more than a musical curiosity, made for the pleasure of the rich. There was no public interest in the piano, and no audience for it. Presumably, Cristofori went back to making harpsichords.

Silbermann finally mastered the Cristofori action and began building *fortepianos* for Frederick the Great, King of Prussia from 1740 to 1786. By 1747, there were fifteen of the instruments in Frederick's collection. A number of harpsichord builders started to make square pianos. Prominent among them were Johann Zumpe, a German living in London; Friedrich Hildebrandt, of Leipzig; and a Swiss, Burkard Tschudi, who had established a harpsichord factory in London in 1742. In 1766 he made some excellent pianos for Frederick the Great. Tschudi's assistant, a Scotsman, John Broadwood, became his son-in-law and then a partner in the firm. Operating today as John Broadwood & Sons, it still makes some of England's finest pianos.

By 1766, Italy, birthplace of the piano, had lost all interest in the instrument. From then on, most piano makers were Germans, Austrians, or other people of Teutonic descent.

The instrument made its first public appearance in a solo concert in 1768, when a Zumpe square piano was played by Johann Christian Bach, youngest son, by a second marriage, of the great Johann Sebastian Bach.

A Zumpe square piano made in London, 1770.

An interior view.

The piano had to battle for an audience; many musicians disliked it, and called it "a noise box where one note drums, another rattles, another buzzes, killing every feeling with hammers." But, in fact, pianos of the late eighteenth century were quite delicate and quiet compared with present-day ones.

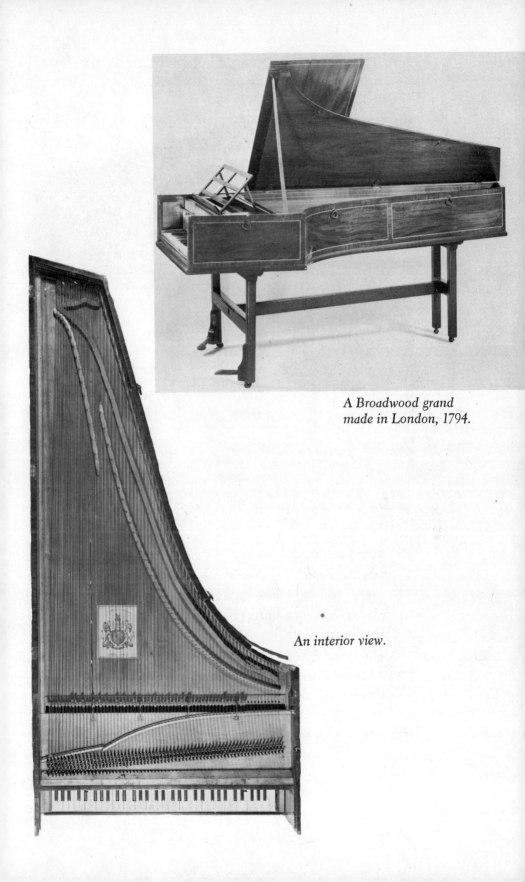

A Broadwood grand
made in London, 1794.

An interior view.

An early grand made by Johann Andreas Stein in Augsburg, 1773.

Fortepiano construction remained as light and elegant as that of the harpsichord.

A giant among piano builders in Europe was Johann Andreas Stein of Augsburg (1728–92), who had been trained by Silbermann. Stein invented a piano mechanism very different from Cristofori's. For the first time in the instrument's history the action was nicely matched to the frame and strings. Performers who had complained of the heavy, deep touch of the Silbermann pianos now delighted in the Stein's shallow, light touch, almost as sensitive as that of a clavichord. The hammers, too, were very light and made blows that the strings could stand up to. The result was a singing tone of great clarity and beauty. Moreover, the power of the trebles was well matched to that of the basses.

Of Stein's piano, Mozart wrote: "I can do with the keys what I like; the tone is always equal; it does not tinkle disagreeably. It has neither the fault of being too loud nor too soft, nor does it fail entirely."

In 1792, at the age of twenty-three, Stein's daughter, Maria Anna, or Nanette, Streicher inherited the family business and soon moved it to Vienna, where for forty years she was considered the empress of the piano-making world. She became a close friend of the great composer Ludwig van Beethoven, supplying him with pianos, watching over his health, and sometimes looking after his household.

A famous cabinetmaker of Germany, Heinrich Engelhard Steinway, made a few pianos on the side. Two years after the German revolution of 1848, a son, Karl (or Charles), a liberal out of favor politically, emigrated to the United States. He got work as a cabinetmaker and soon sent for the rest of the family: his father, mother, three sisters, and his brothers Heinrich, Wilhelm, and Albert. Another brother, Theodor, was left in charge of his own small piano factory in Brunswick, Germany. The father and the sons were all employed in different piano factories in New York until 1853, when they combined as Steinway & Sons. Theodor sold his business in Germany and joined the others as a partner in 1865. Dorette, the eldest daughter, became the New York firm's best piano salesperson, sometimes offering free piano lessons to a prospective buyer in order to make a sale. Today, Steinway & Sons is the world's leading piano manufacturer.

Sebastian Érard (1752–1831), a young Alsatian, made the first piano in France in 1777. His firm was advertised on a

Square piano made by Érard in Paris, 1799.

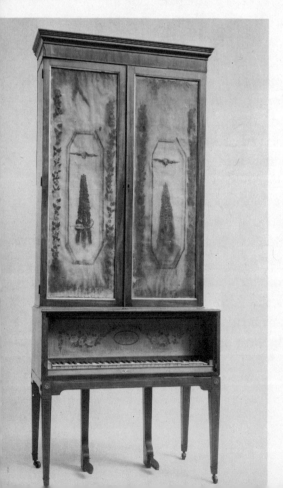

*An early upright
with string tower
made by W. W. Stodart
in London, 1801.*

handbill announcing Franz Liszt's first Parisian concert, when that pianist was only twelve. Another famous early piano maker in France was an Austrian, Ignaz Josef Pleyel, who started in 1807. From 1831 on, Frédéric Chopin, the pianist and composer, made Pleyel pianos world-renowned. The Pleyel and the Érard are still the leading pianos of France.

All these makers except Stein based their designs on the original Cristofori action, and tried to improve the shortcomings of his piano's structure. Its chief fault had been a frame too weak to carry stringings that could withstand perfectly the forceful blows made possible by the new hammer action. Because of this, the intended musical effect often was spoiled. During a concert, a player sometimes had to leave the keyboard in the middle of a piece in order to tune a string or two.

The basic structural weakness was in the gap that is needed across the full width of the soundboard so that the hammers can come up and hit the strings. The problem of strengthening the gap was solved in 1788 by Robert Stodart when he built metal arches from the wrest plank—the board that holds the tuning pins—to the soundboard of his grand pianofortes.

A pioneer in the use of iron combined with wood in piano framing was John Isaac Hawkins, an Englishman and civil engineer. In 1800, at Philadelphia, Pennsylvania, he invented and produced the first upright piano, which he called a portable grand. Hawkins was not the first musical-instrument maker to upend strings. There had been the pyramid and the giraffe pianos. In 1798, William Southwell, an Irish piano maker, produced a square piano with a similar vertical treatment of strings. W. F. Collard of London did the same.

But Hawkins' upright was the first in which strings went clear to the floor, with the keyboard coming at about their midpoint. This factor cut down the instrument's height. Hawkins' new type of piano had several other improvements:

The Hawkins upright piano, made in Philadelphia, 1801.

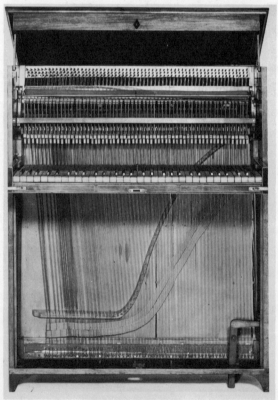

An interior view.

a complete iron frame, independent of its case; a system of resistance rods, combined with an iron upper bridge; and an entirely suspended soundboard.

In 1811, Robert Wornum, in England, produced a diagonally strung short, or cottage, upright—what we now call a spinet—and in 1813, a vertically strung one.

Most of the development of metal-frame construction for pianos took place in America in the 1820's, although James Broadwood, in England, experimented with metal bracing for the trebles of his pianos as early as 1808. The American approach centered on efforts to combine the frame and the reinforcing bars in a single casting, instead of casting or forging them as separate units. In 1833, in Philadelphia, Conrad Meyer successfully made a single-casting resistance

Upright made by Robert Wornum in London, c. 1814.

Square piano made by Stewart & Chickering in Massachusetts, 1823.

frame for a square piano. Meyer's idea was improved upon by Jonas Chickering, of Boston, whose factory was established in 1823. To him is credited the invention of the complete reinforced iron frame for the concert grand. Today, because of his ingenuity, the instrument that only about seventy-five years ago was inclined to buckle and twist under the pull of its strings can stand a strain of almost 20 tons.

The Broadwood Company in England produced its first completely iron-framed grand in 1851. In 1855, the Steinway metal frame made its debut. It was the first full-cast frame for a grand piano with overstringing. Prior to that time, all grands were straight-strung. The Steinway metal frame became the model for all successful frames thereafter.

During the last half of the nineteenth century the piano went far ahead of its rival, the harpsichord, in popularity. Today the harpsichord is played chiefly by a few concert

Square piano made by Steinway & Sons, New York, 1877–78.

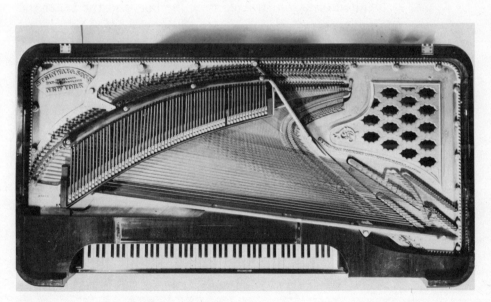

Interior view, showing full cast-metal frame.

performers, although interest in it is again increasing. By 1885, the piano had reached the basic form it still has today.

At the beginning of the twentieth century there were about two hundred independent piano manufacturers in the United States. The peak year for piano sales in the United States was 1909, when 364,545 pianos were bought. The upright player piano, or pianola, was popular at that time. Its music was made mechanically by the player's feet pumping pedals. They worked a bellows that forced air through tubes to a tracker bar. It had eighty-eight holes—one for each of the piano's keys. Whenever a hole came together with one of the holes cut into a music roll being reeled off against the tracker bar, air was released, taking the pressure off a valve. The valve would then put a hammer into action against a string and play a note. The faster the player pumped, the faster the music roll traveled over the bar, and the faster the music played.

But the automobile and the radio came along and took people out of their parlors and away from piano playing. During the 1920's, most of America's piano firms failed. During the Depression 1930's, others either gave up or were swallowed up by two massive combines: the Aeolian Company and the American Piano Company. Today, of about two dozen firms making pianos in the United States, only Baldwin, established in 1862, and Steinway remain as large independents.

5.   How a Piano Is Put Together

The Steinway piano factory, claimed to be the world's foremost, is in Long Island City, New York, just across the East River from Manhattan. It has 400,000 square feet of factory floor space and some four hundred technical workers besides office staff and maintenance employees. The Steinway business is run by the family, with four great-grandsons of the founder, Heinrich Engelhard Steinway, at the factory.

Steinway makes five models of grand piano, and three sizes of upright. Uprights are measured by height—grands by length. The longest Steinway grand is the concert model, measuring 9 feet; the shortest is 5 feet, 1 inch. The smallest upright is 40 inches high; the tallest, 46½ inches.

One of Steinway's fancier grands is No. 300,000, which was presented to the nation in 1938 by the Steinway family in gratitude for its success in America. This piano, whose value is estimated at $50,000, replaced one similarly given in 1903. That piano now is in the Smithsonian Institution. The newer one is in the East Room of the White House, in Washington, D.C. Its gaudy decoration includes an ornamental band of golden figures along one side of the case—singing cowboys, American Indians, Virginia Reel and New England barn dancers. The piano's massive gilded legs are carved to represent eagles with lifted wings, which give the impression that the piano is about to take flight.

The White House piano.

Every honest piano maker prides himself on the smooth action and even sound of his instrument. All notes should work with one another, going easily and harmoniously from the highest to the lowest tones. This result cannot be achieved by assembly-line production. In the Steinway factory each step in the making of a piano is handled by a highly skilled, long-experienced specialist.

It takes a full year to produce a grand piano, which has twelve thousand parts—many of wood, carefully fashioned by hand with the help of specially designed machines. All carving on the piano cases and legs is done by hand.

Many kinds of wood are used: Sitka spruce for sound-boards; yellow poplar for core wood; rock maple for rims and action parts, including hammer shanks; American black walnut and Honduras mahogany for cabinetry; and sugar pine for keys. The lumber is all of the best grade, and is kiln-dried to prevent warping and bending. It is cut selectively, and as much as 40 percent is discarded as unsuitable.

A modern piano factory is a pleasant place to work. It is clean and smells agreeably of the woods and their polishes. To keep piano wood in its best condition, the room temperature and humidity are constantly controlled. So, in winter the factory is pleasantly warm—in summer, ideally cool.

An important wooden part of a grand piano is its rim, shaped like a gigantic letter U that has been dented on one side. The piano rim is formed of as many as twenty-two layers of long hard-maple slats, each three-sixteenths of an inch thick and about twelve inches wide—the depth of the grand piano's case. The strips—wood of the same growth, grade, and texture—are glued together side by side, back to back, into a laminated plank the length and width of the rim. Then, while the glue is still wet, this plank is bent around a monster steel form by manpower, using simple metal lever wrenches and a unique screw-clamp system. It was devised by Theodor Steinway, the founder's son who came last to America; the clamp was patented in 1880. After the rim is in place on the steel form and is firmly held by the clamps, a high-frequency generator sets up a magnetic field between two wide strips of copper plate that hug the rim, back and front. Electric current flows through the wood and dries the glue in only about seven minutes. After that, not even opposing teams of draft horses could pull the strips apart.

The outer surfaces of a piano are veneered—covered with a thin layer of wood. Walnut and mahogany veneers are most

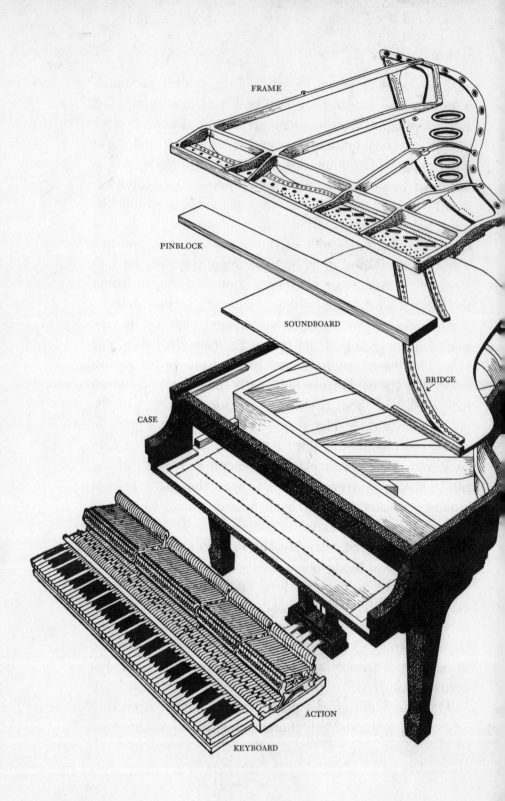

FRAME

PINBLOCK

SOUNDBOARD

BRIDGE

CASE

ACTION

KEYBOARD

often used, and stained to show the grain. For grand pianos, plain mahogany, as an outer veneer, is blackened by lacquer in a process called ebonizing—or making the wood look like ebony, a dark African hardwood. Veneers come in the form called flitch—planklike strips all cut from the same log. The Steinway company keeps all sorts of veneer wood on hand to meet any unusual request: rosewood; cherry; beautifully striped African mahogany; English sycamore; Circassian walnut, from Russia's Black Sea area; birch; oak; maple.

Perhaps the most important part of a piano's basic structure is the metal frame. Steinway grand piano frames weigh about 190 pounds. They are foundry-cast to Steinway specifications by an outside contractor. Holes are drilled in each frame to hold hitch pins and tuning pins for the 240 strings. The frames are lacquered—black first, followed by a golden bronze.

Strings, fitted by hand, are eventually stretched to a tension of 165 pounds each—in all, 39,600 pounds, or almost 20 tons, of stress.

The basic difference in assembling grands and uprights is this: the frame and works of the grand are fitted into its case, but the upright's case is wrapped around its frame and works.

A vital part of both models is the wrest plank, or pin block. It holds the tuning pins and strings at the player's end of the piano. The wrest plank is a long piece of laminated wood

An exploded view of a grand piano. The keyboard and action slide into the front of the case. The soundboard (with bridge attached), pin block, and frame are fitted into the case's top.

—six layers of rock maple—behind the keyboard. The grain of each layer is placed at a 45-degree angle to its mate, to prevent tuning-pin slippage, which can put a piano out of tune very quickly.

The piano's soundboard is built of thin strips of close-grained spruce, carefully glued together to make a resonant surface in the same harp shape as the frame. The grain of the wood is carefully matched to go diagonally across the board along the line of the treble bridge, as vibrations always travel along the grain. The soundboard is eight millimeters thick—about five-sixteenths of an inch—at the center, tapering to five millimeters at the edges. Thirteen braces are glued to it.

Each piano's action is custom-fitted into the case and is given careful checking and delicate adjustment. For instance, the pressure needed to move dampers sideways is measured in grams.

In a grand piano, the action, with hammers glued on, is mounted on a key frame with a set of keys. Then that entire assembly is fitted into the case, adjusted, and regulated. Only after this entire assembly is regulated are the damper mechanisms fitted in behind the key-and-action assembly.

In an upright piano, the action mechanism is mounted inside the piano on the mounting bolts. Then a set of keys is fitted underneath this action mechanism and mounted firmly to the key bottom. After this operation the dampers are fitted in and aligned with the strings prior to gluing the hammers in. Then the whole assembly is regulated.

A piano has twenty-five thousand contact points. Since there can be no oil in the instrument, all moving parts of the action are served by tiny bushings made of the same material as that used in non-stick frying pans. This synthetic material has replaced the wool cloth formerly used.

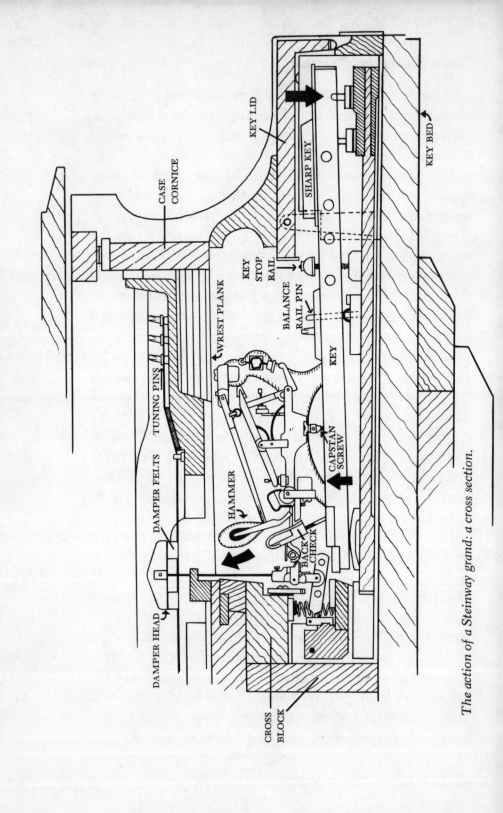

The action of a Steinway grand: a cross section.

The final process of giving the instrument its sound is done by men called voicers, who pierce the pressed-felt heads of the hammers with a four-needled pick to improve the tone. If over-punctured, the felt becomes too soft and makes a muddy tone. Not enough holes make the tone harsh and hard. The voicer must also see that each hammer strikes the string at precisely the right point, with even contact.

The Steinway factory's strangest sight is the "torture machine," a newly developed sort of perpetual-motion affair for loosening up a piano's action. This contrivance is a set of eighty-eight mechanically operated, felt-tipped hammers placed above the piano's keyboard to strike each note in suc-

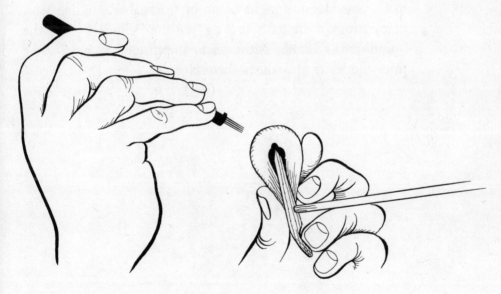

"Voicing" or needling the hammer head to improve the piano tone.

cession—about 250 times a minute. One hour of such intensive playing is said to equal one year of normal piano use, but is even better, for every key is sounded equally.

Key polishing is the last thing done before a piano is sent off in its plastic overcoat to a salesroom. Piano keys no longer are made of ivory from elephants' tusks, but of high-grade plastic. It does not crack, nor does it turn yellow, as ivory does, from the natural oils absorbed from a player's fingers.

In the past fifty years, hundreds of patents have been taken out on new processes of piano manufacture. The greatest advancement was made from 1825 to 1851, when 1,098 piano-improvement patents were granted, mostly in England and France. One of the most useful was Henri Pape's invention, in 1826, of a hammer head of felt, instead of sheepskin, buckskin, flannel, sponge, gutta-percha, or cotton wool. Another significant development was overstringing, which made possible an upright piano of reasonable size and gave bass strings a better vibrating position, directly over the soundboard's center. Most piano improvements have come from the ideas of pianists themselves.

6. Keyboard Notables:
Concert and Jazz

Most piano students are content to become accomplished amateurs, playing the piano only for pleasure. Among the lot are many distinguished people: former President of the United States Harry S. Truman and our present Chief Executive, Richard M. Nixon; many famous authors and journalists; baseball, football, and other sports stars; scientists, poets, painters; actors and actresses, including Katharine Hepburn, Fred Astaire, and Charlie Chaplin.

Applause, fame, fortune, and the satisfaction of giving musical pleasure to others are the reward of the professional concert pianist, but his life is rigidly disciplined. He must be careful of his health, and cannot do anything that might injure his hands. And few professional concert artists ever conquer the nervousness of stepping onstage to face an audience waiting to judge their latest performance in the light of past ones.

Solo work demands the most of a piano player, but to appear in public with other musicians—as an accompanist or a member of an orchestra, band, or other musical group—also requires a great deal of concentration, energy, and stamina.

Although best known as a master of the clavichord, the organ, and the harpsichord, Johann Sebastian Bach did play the piano on at least one auspicious occasion—in a private concert for the King of Prussia, Frederick the Great, at Potsdam in 1747.

The earliest known public performance on the piano was given in England at the Theatre Royal, Covent Garden, on May 16, 1767, when a Miss Brickler sang "a favorite song from *Judith*, accompanied by Mr. Dibdin on a *New Instrument*, called PIANO FORTE." The following year, Johann Christian Bach introduced the piano to the world as a solo concert instrument, in the same city.

Pioneer players of the piano had to forget clavichord-harpsichord technique. This new instrument spoke its own language; it called for a new system of fingering. Johann Sebastian Bach had worked out basic principles of keyboard technique, involving more use of the thumbs and little fingers. In 1753, a son, Carl Philipp Emanuel Bach, published the first really dependable guidebook to fingering. His contribution will be discussed in the following chapter.

Solo piano playing began in earnest in the early 1770's with young Muzio Clementi, the teenage son of an Italian silversmith. Clementi was the pianistic sensation of London, but

Muzio Clementi.

Ladislav Dussek.

he soon had a formidable rival in Wolfgang Amadeus Mozart, who began to concentrate on the piano in 1777, when he was twenty-one.

During the last quarter of the eighteenth century, when pianists were storming public halls, there was a question of which way to sit before an audience. With the back to it? Facing it? Or sideways, and if so, which side? The problem was decided once and for all by the Czech virtuoso, Jan Ladislav Dussek, a performer with a handsome right profile, and very showy right-hand fingering, which he chose to exhibit. Today, following Dussek's example, all pianists sit with their right side facing the audience.

Rivaling Dussek as top pianist of his period were Johann Baptist Cramer, a pupil of Clementi's, and Johann Nepomuk Hummel, a Hungarian musician who had been a protégé of Mozart's. Also prominent were British John Field, Bohemian Ignaz Moscheles, and German Friedrich Kalkbrenner.

Ludwig van Beethoven made his appearance in Vienna in 1792, at twenty-two. He was small, ugly, and pockmarked, but a true pianist. Nobody could play so rapidly or improvise better. And he showed an astounding depth of feeling; there was nothing sweet or sentimental or superficial about his playing. Beethoven was the first of the forceful pianists. In the name of expression he broke all rules—and quite a few pianos. He regarded the piano as an orchestra and attacked it with such gusto as to send strings and hammers flying.

The beginning of the nineteenth century was a fruitful period for romantic pianists. A sterling half-dozen were born within a few years of each other: Felix Mendelssohn, German, 1809; Frédéric Chopin, Polish, 1810; Franz Liszt, Hungarian, 1811; Sigismund Thalberg, Swiss, 1812; Adolf von Henselt, German, 1814; and Alexander Dreyschock, Bohemian, 1818.

Liszt was the greatest pianist of his time, and a real showman. He was breathtakingly handsome, an egomaniac who usually wore a chestful of medals that clanked as he flung himself about the keyboard. Often three pianos were onstage at once. He went from one to the other as strings and hammers broke. When he played, females rushed onstage and instead of bouquets flung their jewels at his feet. They shrieked. They fainted in ecstasy. As mementos, they snatched up stubs of the cigars he had smoked. His broken piano strings were carried away from concerts as priceless souvenirs.

By the mid-century, the piano had become widely accepted. Any family of even slight importance had one. Every young lady of distinction either played the piano or sang with it. Concert pianists became popular idols. Outside of Liszt, the greatest pianist of the day was the Russian virtuoso, Anton Rubinstein (1829–94). A prolific composer and a brilliant improvisor, Rubinstein was king of the concert hall in the decades following the 1850's.

Liszt remained the grand old man of the piano until well into the late nineteenth century, and proved to be a great teacher as well. His pupils included the renowned pianist Arthur Friedheim (1859–1932), the brilliant Moritz Rosen-

Liszt in later years, with Arthur Friedheim.

thal (1862–1946), and the flamboyant Eugen d'Albert (1864–1932). Born in Glasgow, trained in London and Vienna, and later active in Germany as a composer (he wrote 20 operas), d'Albert enjoyed the greatest esteem, even among his fellow virtuosos. According to a story still circulated among musicians, a popular pianist of that day, when asked to name the world's greatest pianist, answered, "Well, I wouldn't presume to name the *first* pianist of the world, but the *second* is surely d'Albert."

Anton Rubinstein.

Ferruccio Busoni.

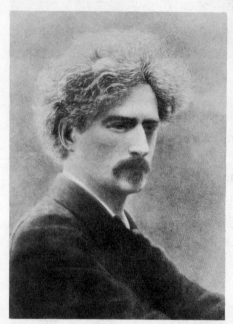

Ignace Jan Paderewski.

There were always new master pianists. Toward the end of the nineteenth century the most prominent pianist was Ignace Jan Paderewski (1860–1941). He was the star pupil of the outstanding piano teacher of the day, an Austrian Pole named Theodor Leschetizky (1830–1915). Young Paderewski became the most admired, the most financially successful, and the most talked-about pianist since Liszt.

Paderewski made his official debut in Vienna in 1887, at twenty-seven. Billed as "the lion of Paris and London," because of his mop of long golden-red hair, he arrived in

America in 1891. He became the biggest concert attraction New York had ever seen. Just to be close to him, a thousand people would clamber onstage after a concert. Crowds waited for hours at railroad stations to see his private railway car flash by. Mobs lined the street from his hotel to the concert hall.

In 1919, Paderewski became prime minister of his native land, Poland. Throughout his life he was an ardent patriot and gave much of his concert earnings to the cause of Polish freedom. His body remains entombed in Arlington National Cemetery, in Washington, D.C., in a vault beneath the memorial to the seamen of the battleship *Maine*, awaiting return to a Poland free of communism.

The concert circuit has had its keyboard clowns, such as Vladimir de Pachmann (1843–1933), who during recitals muttered, made faces, and lectured his audiences. Many considered de Pachmann the greatest living player of Chopin; many others did not. One New York critic went so far as to dub de Pachmann "the Chopinzee." He received backstage visitors in a horrible old bathrobe, which he claimed had belonged to Chopin. Whenever it wore out, another, also credited to Chopin, would take its place. On vacations, de Pachmann made a point of milking cows, claiming that it was the best finger exercise for a pianist.

Perhaps the most intellectual pianist was an Italian, Ferruccio Busoni (1866–1924), a contemporary of Paderewski's. He was the composer of many musical works and was renowned for his brilliant piano technique.

The first lady of America's pianists was Julie Rivé-King (1857–1937), who gave over four hundred solo recitals and played more than five hundred times with orchestras. Following her came Fannie Bloomfield Zeisler (1863–1927), an American born in Austria, who had a vast repertory. She once gave eight recitals in eighteen days, without repeating a number. The female piano star of the latter half of the nineteenth century was German Clara Schumann (1819–96), Liszt's greatest enemy and Brahms's staunchest champion. And there was Liszt's favorite pupil, Sophie Menter (1846–1917), a prima donna with a robust, electrifying style. The most beautiful female pianist may have been young Teresa Carreño (1853–1917), a Venezuelan. She played for President Lincoln in the White House and improvised on his favorite piece, "Listen to the Mocking Bird." (She also complained about the piano.) In later years, she married Eugen d'Albert.

In the first half of our own century, three great ladies of the keyboard were the Englishwoman Myra Hess (1890–1965), Rumanian-born Clara Haskil (1895–1960), and the Polish Wanda Landowska (1877–1959), who, in mid-career, turned to the harpsichord.

After the turn of the twentieth century the pianists' pianist was Leopold Godowsky (1870–1938), a short, plump, round-faced Pole. A down-to-earth concert pianist of that time was Josef Hofmann (1876–1957), a Polish player who had been a child prodigy during the heyday of Paderewski. Hofmann became close friends with another pianist who had captured the public's imagination—Sergei Rachmaninoff (1873–1943), a tall, dour, lank, Russian composer, with a long, deeply lined face, close-cropped hair, and enormous hands. He was a pianist of cool control—a stunning technician.

Other great pianists at the beginning of the twentieth century included Ossip Gabrilowitsch (1878–1936), Harold Bauer (1873–1951), Josef Lhévinne (1874–1944), and his wife Rosina (1880–   ).

They were followed by Alfred Cortot (1877–1962), Rudolph Ganz (1877–   ), Robert Casadesus (1899–   ), Alexander Brailowsky (1896–   ), and the great Beethoven

*Teresa Carreño
as a young girl;
from a photo taken by
Matthew Brady.*

Dame Myra Hess.

*Wanda
Landowska.*

Sergei Rachmaninoff.

interpreter, Artur Schnabel (1882–1951). Most of these artists performed in the 1950's and two of them—Brailowsky and Casadesus—were still giving recitals when this was written.

Many of the earlier piano masters, including those from the turn of the century, have left a record of their performances. These have been transcribed onto modern-day records from earlier recordings, cylinders, and piano rolls. In this way, anyone can hear Leopold Godowsky at the height of his powers, or Sergei Rachmaninoff playing his own compositions.

Vladimir Horowitz, born at Kiev, Russia, in 1904, and still actively performing, is considered by many to be the king of concert pianists of our time. He is a virtuoso pianist, a great *bravura* player and romantic successor to Liszt. At the same time, he is an outstanding interpreter of eighteenth-century piano literature.

The dean of the concert pianists in America today is Artur Rubinstein. Although he was acclaimed all over Europe before coming to the United States during the concert season of 1905–06, Americans who heard him judged him at first to be cold and unemotional. An eminent concert impresario said of Rubinstein's early American failure: "It is not infrequently the fate of great men to be first spurned, then worshiped. Their very uniqueness, the qualities that make them memorable, frighten conservative folk away from them at first."

Rubinstein himself explains his failure differently. "I was lazy," he says. "I had talent, but there were many things in life more important than practicing. I dropped many notes in those days, maybe thirty percent. I was spoiled, and I admit it." (Rubinstein, incidentally, is not related to the earlier Anton Rubinstein.)

Although he has played before the public for about seventy-five years, Rubinstein does not yet hold the record as

Artur Rubinstein.

the longest-performing concert pianist. Camille Saint-Saëns (1835–1921) began when he was five years old, and played professionally at the keyboard for eighty-one years. Isidor Philipp played a concert in New York when he was ninety-three. He celebrated his ninetieth birthday by giving one recital in the afternoon, another in the evening. German-born Wilhelm Backhaus (1884–1969), a Beethoven interpreter of international renown, was still concertizing and recording at age eighty-five.

One of the exciting personalities of the piano concert world in recent times is Van Cliburn, a tall, lean young Texan with a captivating manner. In 1958 he entered the Moscow International Tchaikovsky Piano Competition. Day-to-day news reports built suspense as he went on to win. Wide publicity resulted. Van Cliburn came home triumphantly to a ticker-tape parade up Broadway, a raise in his concert fees, and a name known from coast to coast. But the greatest effect of his victory was to make people in America conscious of piano competitions. The public had never paid much attention to the many exceptionally talented young pianists who had been aided during the preceding several decades by American competitions. Now everyone suddenly took notice.

The major piano competitions in the United States are those financed by the Walter W. Naumburg Musical Foundation, the Edgar M. Leventritt Foundation, and the Quadrennial Van Cliburn Competition (in Fort Worth, Texas). Among Naumburg winners have been William Kapell, Leonid Hambro, Constance Keene, Joseph Schwartz, Abbey Simon, Zadel Skolovsky, and Ralph Votapek. Leventritt awards have gone to Michel Block, John Browning, Van Cliburn, Malcolm Frager, Gary Graffman, Eugene Istomin, Jeffrey Siegel, and Joseph Kalichstein. All of these players have gone on to become concert pianists of renown.

Sviatoslav Richter.   *André Watts.*

The list of master pianists playing the international concert circuit also includes the Russian Sviatoslav Richter, the Italian Arturo Benedetti Michelangeli, the Chilean Claudio Arrau, and the Englishman, Clifford Curzon.

Other sparkling concert pianists of this last half of the twentieth century include young Peter Serkin, son of the famous pianist Rudolf Serkin; André Watts; the controversial Canadian, Glenn Gould; and Jeanne-Marie Darré, known for dazzling interpretations of Chopin's *Études*. A few more are Daniel Barenboim, Philip Evans, Byron Janis, Grant Johannesen, Leo Smit, David Tudor, Rosalyn Tureck, Alicia de Larrocha, Earl Wild, Gina Bachauer, the great Mozart pianist Lili Kraus, and the Brazilian Guiomar Novaes.

Young pianists continue to come from abroad. In 1969, a nineteen-year-old Russian girl, Elena Gilels, the talented daughter of famed pianist Emil Gilels, made her American debut with the Moscow State Symphony at Carnegie Hall. The outstanding young Russian pianist is Vladimir Ashkenazy. From Japan is Yuji Takahashi, born in 1938. He has performed at the Berkshire Music Festival and appeared with the London, Toronto, Boston, and New York symphony orchestras. South America has contributed its share of young performers, including Martha Argerich and Nelson Freire.

The history of piano playing has had its share of tragedy, too. Concertgoers who remember the 1940's and early 1950's still think of Dinu Lipatti, the beloved young Rumanian pianist who died of leukemia at thirty-three, and William Kapell, the young American whose brilliant career ended in a fatal plane crash. The records they made, however, are still being bought by music lovers throughout the world.

During its climb to a position of eminence on the concert stage the piano has not been neglected by other performers. It has always been a favored instrument in taverns, nightclubs, variety acts, and on TV. Victor Borge, a Danish comedian, uses the piano as a foil for his dry wit. Some of the funniest circus-clown acts are based on trick pianos. Many an otherwise dull movie has been saved by piano music. Such comics as the Marx Brothers and Laurel and Hardy created big laughs with the piano. So does Jimmy Durante.

The piano entered the jazz scene early in the century. Its bass tones lent themselves well to an insistent beat. But that need of a definite beat was what kept the piano from becoming a totally effective solo jazz instrument. Because the left hand was kept from roaming the keys, the virtuosity of solo keyboard performers was stunted. A good many jazz-piano geniuses have developed, but many still do their finest work when backed by drums to furnish the necessary beat.

The earliest master jazz pianist was the Black musician, Jelly Roll Morton, born about 1885. His real name was Ferdinand Joseph La Menthe. He had been greatly influenced by Verdi, Massenet, and Donizetti, whose operas he had seen as a boy in the Old French Opera House in New Orleans. But most of all, he was influenced by the music made by the Black men and women of his native city.

After Morton came James P. Johnson, known as a ragtime pianist. Ragtime piano had stiffer syncopation than jazz, with little or no improvisation. Other great jazz pianists have been Earl "Fatha" Hines, Meade Lux Lewis, Joe Sullivan, Thomas

Jelly Roll Morton. *Earl "Fatha" Hines.*

"Fats" Waller, Teddy Weatherford, Sonny White, Thelonious Monk, and Art Tatum.

Some of the top popular pianists today are Oscar Peterson, Bill Evans, Erroll Garner, Herbie Hancock, and Hank Jones. Others are Dave Brubeck, Ahmad Jamal, Ramsey Lewis, Sergio Mendes, and Cecil Taylor. Some great old-timers who are still performing are Count Basie, Ray Charles, and Duke Ellington. Billy Taylor has devoted much time and energy to bringing live music to New York schoolchildren.

All these pianists, both classical and jazz, are worth listening to and learning from.

Thelonious Monk.   *Duke Ellington.*

7. Piano Music and Its Composers

You will enjoy a piano concert more if you know how to listen to the music. Listening with intelligence and appreciation is an ability you must develop for yourself, although someone else or a written commentary can help you to identify certain passages in a composition. Recognizing and being able to evaluate the various technical qualities of the music is the means of comprehending the art being expressed by the composer and the performer.

To understand music, listen and keep on listening. Listen to the same piece over and over until it speaks to you. Try to feel what the composer had in mind. Does he mean to be funny or sad, sweet, sour, gentle, or harsh? Is he speaking of weakness, strength, cruelty, or compassion? What was he thinking of? Love, tenderness, grandeur, despair, revolution, piety, fury, and a long list of other abstractions can all be expressed by music.

Remember: music is not just for the intellect, but also for the senses. Feel music emotionally. Let it flow through you.

Each composer for the piano has written music in his own personal style and usually in that of his period. Each requires a different approach to the hammer action and pedaling. These are things to listen for when you attend a concert.

Observe how different composers and pianists make use of the many factors of musical tone: its pitch (its highness or lowness); its duration (its longness or shortness); its intensity (its softness or loudness); and its timbre (or tone color).

A composer makes music by arranging notes in patterns of time. Try to follow the melody, the particular way the notes follow one another. Seek out the rhythm, the regular occurrence of beat. Feel the tempo, the rate of speed at which a rhythmic pattern is played. Composers mark their music with directions for tempo: *adagio*, very slow; *andante*, moderate speed; *allegro*, fast; *vivace*, lively and faster; *presto*, very fast; and *prestissimo*, as fast as can be performed. These words of direction have been adopted from the Italian language.

Look for the harmony—the way chords are arranged. Chords are tone patterns made by playing three or more notes at the same time. There are consonant chords, made of notes at certain intervals, which sound harmonically satisfying, and there are dissonant chords, made of notes at certain other intervals, which sound restless and unresolved, as if something more should be said.

All music is written to some form. Each piece has its own master plan for holding together melody, rhythm, tempo, and harmony. The form may be a symphony, an opera, a sonata, a concerto, a duet, a trio, a quartet, a quintet, a simple love song, or something else. Note how, in whatever form, the patterns of melody, rhythm, and harmony repeat, and how they contrast.

The musical form most often employed in a solo concert is the sonata, a type of composition developed during the seventeenth and eighteenth centuries, usually written for one or two instruments and generally consisting of three or four contrasting sections, called movements. A pianist appearing with an orchestra, however, will probably play a concerto, a composition for orchestra and one or more solo instruments.

Usually a concerto has three movements. Traditionally the

first is fast and expresses themes, or melodic patterns. Just before this first movement ends, there is a brilliant solo called a cadenza, sometimes written or improvised by the soloist himself. A concerto's second movement is slow and lyrical. The closing movement is lively, often in rondo form—that is, with sections that repeat themselves, alternating with other themes.

Johann Sebastian Bach (1685–1750) and George Frideric Handel (1685–1759) both composed concertos for solo keyboard instruments with orchestra. But Bach had a harpsichordist in mind when he wrote his concertos, and Handel, an organist. Although Bach, as mentioned earlier, contributed notably to the development of fingering techniques for the organ, harpsichord, and clavichord, a satisfactory piano was developed too late in his career to be anything but a novelty to the old composer. At the same time, most of his keyboard works were later absorbed into the piano literature. The same is true of many works by Handel as well as Bach, and by their Neapolitan contemporary, Domenico Scarlatti (1685–1757).

George Frideric Handel.   *Domenico Scarlatti.*

Johann Sebastian Bach.

Carl Philipp Emanuel Bach.

Johann Christian Bach.

It was left to another generation of Bachs—notably Sebastian's eldest son, Carl Philipp Emanuel (1714–88) —to pioneer methods of composing and performing that were really suited to the new instrument. A prolific composer who wrote 210 solo works for keyboard instruments alone, the younger Bach was also the author of the *Essay on the True*

Art of Playing Keyboard Instruments, the guide mentioned in Chapter 6. This was a monumental summing up of keyboard technique that influenced every important pianist-composer—including Mozart and Beethoven—up to the end of the eighteenth century.

Carl Philipp Emanuel's youngest brother, Johann Christian (1735–82), gave piano recitals in London (see page 66). While less influential than Carl Philipp Emanuel, this British-based Bach turned out many works for the piano as well as for the older and still popular harpsichord.

Many of the men who played the piano in concert during the instrument's early days also composed for it. This trend has continued, to a limited extent, into the present day. In the preceding chapter, we discussed Clementi, Mozart, Beethoven, Chopin, Liszt, Anton Rubinstein, Paderewski, Busoni, and Rachmaninoff as public performers. In modern times, the great composer-pianists have included Sergei Prokofiev, Béla Bartók, Dmitri Shostakovich, and Igor Stravinsky.

The first music composed especially for piano appeared in 1732, when twelve sonatas for *Cimbalo di piano e forte* were created by Lodovico Giustino of Pistoia. Franz Joseph Haydn, active as a professional musician from about 1750 until his death in 1809, developed the sonata form on the foundations laid by some of his predecessors. He wrote fifty-two sonatas. Their rondos are remarkably gay and spirited.

The next composer of stature to write for the piano was the Italian Muzio Clementi (1752–1832). A great teacher and a great pianist, he composed sixty sonatas and many sonatinas, shorter and simpler than sonatas, and lively and full of charming ideas.

But it was the Austrian Wolfgang Amadeus Mozart (1756–91) who did more to develop piano music than any other composer of the eighteenth century. Mozart produced

Wolfgang Amadeus Mozart.

his first piano concerto when he was eleven, and he wrote many more, the last in the year of his death. In addition, he wrote a concerto for two pianos, and one for three. Mozart wrote his first big concerto, in E-flat Major, when he was twenty-one. It is neatly done, with nicely judged, full, rich sound; the soloist is carried along by the orchestra and then thrillingly wings off on his own. The music is a grand statement of youth liberating itself. In Mozart's piano concertos, listen for the beautiful teamwork of the piano and the orchestra, the sparkling melody, and the imaginative ornamentation.

Though Mozart paired the piano happily with the orchestra, it took the mighty genius of Beethoven (1770–1827) to lift the piano concerto to its fuller symphonic possibilities. He gave the music an exuberance that showed the piano to best advantage. In the Concerto in C Minor, opus 37, written in 1800—his third piano concerto of five—Beethoven broke with tradition by putting the orchestra on a more equal footing with the soloist, so that the piano in this piece does not soar above the mass of instruments and dominate them.

Franz Peter Schubert (1797–1828), whose short life of thirty-one years fell during Beethoven's time, wrote two large volumes of four-hand piano music, though he composed no concertos. Beginners will find two of his *Eight Impromptus*—in G, opus 90, No. 3, and in A-flat, opus 142, No. 2—especially attractive, as the finger work is easy. Schubert also wrote some stunning piano sonatas. The Sonata in B-flat, opus 960, is the grandest of all. Most played is the *Wanderer Fantasie*, opus 15—stormy, but with sunshine breaking through. It has few equals in emotional effect; the stirring sweep of the last Allegro is unforgettable.

Franz Liszt (1811–86) composed hundreds of works for the piano, including études, Hungarian rhapsodies, piano concertos, sonatas, and fantasias, the last based on melodies drawn from the popular operas of the day. His transcriptions of works by other composers are brilliant, difficult to play, and designed to draw cheers from an audience.

Ludwig van Beethoven.

In 1818, there appeared on the concert stage a nine-year-old piano prodigy, Jakob Ludwig Felix Mendelssohn-Bartholdy, better known as Felix Mendelssohn. By the time young Felix was twelve, he had composed sixty musical works, many of them for piano. Mendelssohn's particular bent was for delicate, sparkling music, with notes darting about as if on gossamer wings. This quality first appeared when he was sixteen, in his remarkable Piano Quartet in B Minor, opus 3.

Probably Mendelssohn's best-known piano work is the *Rondo Capriccioso* in E, opus 14. His forty-eight *Songs Without Words* are a treasure chest for amateur pianists. The best known of his five piano concertos is the one in G Minor, opus 25.

No one has written more colorful piano pieces than Frédéric Chopin (1810–49), born in Poland a year after Mendelssohn. Chopin composed 172 piano solos, including fifty-one mazurkas, inspired by the Polish dances of that name, and nineteen nocturnes—dreamy, pensive compositions. In Chopin's *Black Key Étude* the thumb was used on black keys for the first time.

A tragic contemporary of Chopin's was Robert Schumann (1810–56), husband of the famous Clara Schumann. His work is superbly melodic and has rich emotional power and strange magical charm. Schumann was forced to give up a promising concert career when his right hand became crippled for life through the use of a mechanical gadget intended to strengthen his weak fourth finger. In his lovely piano concerto, Schumann achieved an unprecedented blend of piano and orchestral sound.

The influence of Schumann and Mendelssohn was felt as far away as Scandinavia. There, the Norwegian Edvard Grieg (1843–1907) wrote sonatas, piano miniatures, Norwegian

Frédéric Chopin.

Robert and Clara Schumann.

dances, and the mighty Piano Concerto in A Minor—one of the most popular concert pieces of all time.

One of the most fascinating musician-composer personalities of the nineteenth century was Louis Moreau Gottschalk (1829–69). Born in New Orleans of a Creole mother, he was

Edvard Grieg.

Louis Moreau Gottschalk.

an infant prodigy and began the study of the piano in Paris when he was thirteen. He became a student of Berlioz and was the first of America's musical matinee idols. P. T. Barnum offered Gottschalk twenty thousand dollars to make a concert tour. He presented eighty concerts in New York City and almost one thousand in Latin America, where he was known as "the first musical ambassador from the United States."

In the late nineteenth century, the New England composer-pianist Edward MacDowell (1861–1908) was America's musical ambassador to Europe. His charming piano cycle, Woodland Sketches, has remained popular with students, but MacDowell was also capable of composing in the grand manner. His romantic second piano concerto has been revived with great success by modern concert pianists.

The German composer Johannes Brahms (1833–97) was a talented pianist. Equally renowned as a composer of symphonies, string quartets, and choral works, Brahms produced a large body of compositions for the piano throughout his long career. Brahms used the piano in every possible way—as a solo instrument; accompanying a violin, cello, or singing voice; combining with a horn and violin in a trio, or with string instruments in a quartet or quintet. He could write charming, intimate piano works that were truly "chamber music" and he could write powerful concertos that continue to challenge today's virtuosos. The second of his two piano concertos, for instance, is a full-blown symphony for piano and orchestra.

Two notable French piano composers whose lives extended into the twentieth century are Camille Saint-Saëns (1835–1921) and Claude Debussy (1862–1918).

Young pianists will enjoy Saint-Saëns' Danse Macabre (Dance of Death), opus 40, and his Carnaval des Animaux,

Edward MacDowell.

Grande Fantasie Zoologique (Carnival of the Animals, Grand Zoological Fantasy). The animal piece is great fun, with piano imitations of a lion's roar, crowing roosters and cackling hens, a donkey's bray, leaping kangaroos, and a waltzing elephant.

Debussy's music is modern in feeling. It suggests moods and impressions. His harmonies are often dissonant and the music sounds strange at first hearing. But it is full of poetry and mystery. His *Preludes for Piano* cast a haunting spell on the listener.

Maurice Ravel (1875–1937) also wrote music with a modern feeling, but it does not have the dreamy effect of Debussy's work. Ravel wrote numerous charming and simple

Maurice Ravel.

piano pieces. He loved children, animals (especially cats), fairy tales, mechanical toys, American jazz, and Spanish fla- mencos. An interesting Ravel work is his *Concerto in D for the Left Hand*. This was composed especially for a pianist who had lost his right arm in World War I, but who wished to resume his concert career. Ravel and several other com- posers cooperated by writing pieces for him to play.

As the new century began, composers took new directions and upset many accepted ideas of melody, rhythm, and harmony. One of the early American musical radicals was Charles Ives (1874–1954). A graduate of Yale, where he had studied composition, Ives found little or no popular acceptance of his music. Forced by necessity to take up a business career, Ives lived a double life—as one of two partners heading a successful insurance agency, and as an inspired composer whose works were fifty years ahead of their time. His piano rhythms are incredibly complex, with weird chord formations and dissonances. His works often make use of the old hymn tunes and marching pieces that he remembered from his New England childhood.

In 1912, a young Californian, Henry Cowell, composed piano music that called for tone clusters, produced by striking the piano keys with the fist, the palms of the hands, the pointed fingers, the elbow, and the forearm.

Some noted American piano composers of the 1920's were Roy Harris, Roger Sessions, Virgil Thomson, and Deems Taylor. In Paris, Alexander Tcherepnin experimented with modified oriental scales and with the concept of a new scale using nine tones instead of the traditional eight.

Perhaps the most important man of the new music was Arnold Schönberg (1874–1951). His experiments can be sampled in three early twentieth-century works: *Three Piano*

Béla Bartók.   Sergei Prokofiev.

Pieces, opus 11; *Six Little Piano Pieces*, opus 19; and *Piano Suites*, opuses 23 and 25.

Béla Bartók (1881–1945), a Hungarian, came closest to matching piano satisfactorily with the modern full orchestra, and forced a fresh look at the piano as a percussive instrument. In his orchestral works the piano and the drums work out a marvelously close relationship. For piano teaching, Bartók wrote a set of 153 folk dances, growing progressively more difficult, called *Mikrokosmos*. They include pleasant five-finger exercises.

Out of Russia came two towering composers whose work has left an indelible mark on piano literature: Igor Stravinsky (1882–   ) and Sergei Prokofiev (1891–1953).

A momentous piano event of 1924 was the introduction by Paul Whiteman's jazz symphony orchestra of George Gershwin's now famous piano concerto, *Rhapsody in Blue*. This was an attempt to adapt the jazz style to a concert piece.

Later, in the 1930's, came the work of Samuel Barber,

Igor Stravinsky.

Abram Chasins, Aaron Copland, William Schuman, and Gian Carlo Menotti. Menotti's *Poemetti* are delightful piano pieces for young people.

Copland used cowboy tunes for his two-piano suite for the ballet, *Billy the Kid*, and wrote some lively piano music for children.

John Cage is perhaps the most radical current composer for piano. His specialty is the "prepared piano," in which screws, rubber bands, and small objects are attached to strings to achieve various sound effects. Cage has many followers, among them a Japanese pianist, Toshi Ichyanagi.

In the 1960's, the world's outstanding player of Cage's music, and of all avant-garde piano, has been David Tudor, also a brilliant orthodox pianist. A piano concert by Tudor is an event—a happening. He hits the keyboard, raps the soundboard from below, leans into the piano to sweep its strings, blows a whistle or kazoo, and controls the playing of several tape recorders—or sometimes merely sits and stares at the keys, as he does in an oddly named number, *4'33"* (*Four Minutes, Thirty-three Seconds*), a work of timed silences, composed by John Cage.

8. The Care of Your Piano

A piano is sensitive. Take good care of yours. Do not place it where there will be extremes of temperature. Cold and heat are hard on a piano's mechanism because the instrument's materials—wood, metal, wire, felt, plastic—contract and expand at varying rates during temperature changes.

In extremely hot, dry weather a piano's wood may shrink and cause the soundboard to split and the screws in the action to loosen. Loud reports that sound like rifle shots, heard during such a time, should be investigated immediately. Electrical humidity-control gadgets are available; if placed inside a piano, they will prevent such damage.

A patio or a porch is a poor spot for a piano, as sunlight damages the finish. A bedroom is unsuitable, because a window usually is opened there at night. A basement playroom with a cement or earthen floor is bad, as dampness is ruinous to a piano.

See that a·furnace is not too close at hand, and screen off any other heatmakers that are near a piano. For the screen, use nonconducting material: plywood, plasterboard, or cloth stretched on a frame.

The ideally shaped room for a piano is two-thirds longer than it is wide, with its height somewhat more than its width. To get the best sound from your piano, keep it away from walls. They can make unpleasant echoes. Put the instrument as far into the room as possible, so that the floor can serve as an extra sounding board. Draperies, carpets, and matting tend to deaden a piano's tone.

Protect your piano from air currents. Do not put it between two windows, or a door and a window, where rain may enter it. Water or any other liquid inside a piano is disastrous. Beware of air conditioning. Units that are turned on and off from time to time can be damaging to a piano.

Keep the piano keyboard fairly clean. Wipe the keys with a damp cloth occasionally, but be careful that water does not get down between them. Cover the keys when the piano is not in use. During a rainy spell the keys may stick if the piano is not kept reasonably warm.

Try to keep dust out of the piano. Gently vacuum it once in a while. When a grand piano is not being played, keep its lid down. Do not put things on top of it, and be sure that small objects do not fall in among the strings. Even something as small as a pin can make a disagreeable whizzing or jingling when the piano is played.

Keep your piano always at the recognized standard pitch, which is 440 vibrations per second on the A above middle C. It is commonly called the 440-A. Strings tighten and become sharp in cold weather, and loosen and become flat in hot weather. Have your piano tuned once every six weeks, if it is played much. Some tuners who claim to know their work do not do a thorough job, so be sure to get a tuner who is recommended by a reliable person—a piano dealer or your teacher, perhaps. Or find someone who is a member of the Piano Technicians Guild, a national organization of piano tuners.

Good care of your piano will ensure that it is always ready in top-notch condition when you wish to play it.

Finale

Your first reward from piano playing will be the satisfaction of having mastered the instrument. All the hours of practice, the finger stretchings and muscle aches, will be forgotten, once you have learned really to play your piano.

A famous writer, Sherwood Anderson, once said, "The point of being an artist is that you may live." By becoming acquainted with your keyboard, you will have learned to live a bit more than you did before.

Once you yourself have conquered the technical problems, you will begin genuinely to appreciate the artistry of professional concert pianists. You will be amazed at how much more pleasure a concert will give you.

A pleasant pastime, or an absorbing hobby, can be reading about the piano and about the lives of famous pianists and piano composers, past and present. Keep scrapbooks of the artists whom you hear. Save programs of concerts, so that you will remember them better. Buy records of the pieces you have heard played. Listen to them carefully so that you will gain new understanding of the music. With records, you can stage piano recitals right in your own living room.

Being able to play the piano will take you out among people. You will make new friends—boys and girls, men and women, who feel the same as you do about many things. You will have more to talk about, more to think about. The better you play, the wider may be your circle of friends.

No longer will you be a music spectator, but a player. Join your school orchestra and learn the joy and discipline of being a member of a musical group. Learn to play four-hand piano with a friend. You'll enjoy it.

Try to go to a summer music camp at the seashore, in lake country, or in the mountains. Young people at these camps study music with professionals and play their instruments with students of their own age and proficiency. And there is plenty of time to enjoy swimming, hiking, cookouts, tennis, horseback riding, and all the other delights of the outdoors. A book called *A Parent's Guide to Music Lessons*, by Wills and Manners (Harper & Row), carries a handy listing of more than two hundred of these music camps, located in forty-six states. Many of them are in California, Texas, and Illinois, but there is even one in Alaska. Up-to-date listings of music camps can be had from the Association of Private Camps, 55 West 42nd Street, New York, N.Y., or the American Camping Association, 342 Madison Avenue, New York, N.Y.

With a few friends of your neighborhood, you could form a chamber-music group. But be warned: playing music with others can be great pleasure, or great dissatisfaction. Be careful in choosing your companions; find amiable players who are just as serious about music as you are. A small ensemble will teach each of you a tolerance of the viewpoints of others and something about the give-and-take of life.

Your group might become good enough to get paying engagements at local club meetings, dinners and luncheons, political rallies, and other gatherings. Perhaps you could offer your services to play piano for children's hospitals and old folks' homes. People in such institutions seldom hear live music.

Although composition is a major musical field in itself, you might like to make up a few tunes of your own on the piano. Try writing some music, and playing it.

You may be gifted enough and willing to work hard enough to make piano playing your career. Remember that behind every successful professional concert pianist lie long years of labor, endurance, and patience. But should you succeed as a concert artist, the rewards will be well worth your effort. Be sure to get the best teacher you can.

Whether you play professionally or just for pleasure, you will bring beauty to yourself and the world. Art in any form is a measure of companionship. Music is no exception.

Charles Cooke, a famous magazine writer and amateur pianist, has said, "Every piano, upright or grand, long owned or newly bought, is literally a treasure chest, waiting to give forth its inexhaustible gifts to elevate and enrich the lives around it."

No truer words will ever be written.

Glossary

Action—The operation of a piano's keys and hammers against its strings.

Adagio—Slow, an indication of tempo used as a playing direction in music.

Allegro—Fast, lively, an indication of tempo used as a playing direction in music.

Andante—Going, moving, a moderate tempo—used as a playing direction in music.

Avant-garde—That which is ahead of popular taste.

Cadenza—In a concerto, a brilliant, unaccompanied solo section, once improvised by the player, now more often already composed. It enlarges on the themes set forth in the work and exhibits the player's technique.

Capotasto, or captasto, bar—Of a piano, a heavy metal bar that bridges the strings just before they tie off at the tuning pins. It keeps the strings in place, much as the fingerboard nut on a violin does. *Capotasto* means "head" (*capo*) of "key" or "tapper" (*tasto*).

Capriccio—A short, whimsical musical piece that is free in form and usually lively in style. Also called *caprice*.

Chamber music—Music that has a small number of players, usually one to a part. It was originally intended to be played in a small space such as a room in a house, instead of in a church, theater, or concert hall.

CHORD—A tone pattern made by playing three or more notes at the same time. *Consonant* chords, made up of tones at certain intervals, are restful ones that seem to say the final word. *Dissonant* chords, made up of tones at certain other intervals, sound restless and incomplete, demanding something more to be said.

CHORDOPHONE—A musical instrument that makes its sound by a vibrating string.

CLAVICHORD—From *clavis*, Greek for "key," and "*chord*," a "string." A keyboard stringed musical instrument played by the tangent, or touch, action of small brass wedges striking the strings.

CONCERTO—A large-scale musical composition, putting together an orchestra and one or more solo instruments. The word comes from the Latin *concertare: con*, meaning "with," and *certare*, meaning "to strive"—the whole meaning "to strive with."

DAMPER—A felt-topped strip of wood that, when in place on a piano string, keeps it from vibrating.

DULCIMER—A stringed instrument that came to Europe from the East during the Middle Ages. Its strings are struck with hammers held in the hands.

DYNAMICS—Degrees of loudness or softness in a musical performance.

ESCAPEMENT—The mechanism in a piano that allows the hammer to "escape" after a string has been struck, so leaving the string to vibrate. Double escapement allows a hammer to strike a second time without waiting for the key to rise to its normal position of rest.

ÉTUDE—A study—hence, a piece of music meant to give practice in instrumental technique.

FANTASIA—A musical piece in which the composer has not been bound to any conventional form.

FLAMENCO—A Spanish gypsy song or dance.

FLITCH—A plank-sized chunk of lumber that has been cut into very thin slices for veneering piano cases.

FORM—The master plan for holding together melody, rhythm, tempo, and harmony to make a musical composition—be it symphony, opera, sonata, concerto, duet, trio, quartet, quintet, or whatever. The basic elements in musical form are repetition, variation, and contrast.

FRAME—Of a piano, the skeleton of cast iron on which the strings are stretched.

HAMMER—Of a piano, that part of the mechanism that strikes the strings to produce the tone: a wooden shaft with a compressed-felt tip.

HARMONY—The way in which chords are arranged in a musical composition.

HARPSICHORD—A plucked-string keyboard musical instrument. The strings are made to vibrate by being plucked by plectra, or picks, of raven's quill or leather.

HIGH FREQUENCY—Fast vibrations that make a tone of high pitch.

HITCH PIN—Of a piano, a metal pin inserted tightly in the frame to hold one end of a string; the other end is attached to a tuning pin.

KEYBOARD—Of a piano, the eighty-eight black and white keys that connect to the instrument's action.

LOW FREQUENCY—Slow vibrations that make a tone of low pitch.

MAZURKA—A lively Polish dance in triple time.

MELODY—A parade of notes, one following the other meaningfully.

MINUET—A slow, stately seventeenth-century French dance for groups of couples; written in triple time.

MONOCHORD—An ancient Greek one-string musical instrument, consisting of a single gut or metal string stretched between two bridges resting on a sound box, with a third bridge to be moved along under the taut string to predetermined points, in order to demonstrate fundamental laws of harmonics and to teach pitch.

MUSICAL BOW—A primitive musical instrument, made of a stick bent by the tension of a thong, which makes a musical tone when twanged or hammered. There are two types of musical bow: one with an attached resonator, or sound box; one with a separate resonator. In some cases, the resonator is formed by the open mouth of the player.

OCTAVE—A succession of eight notes comprising a scale, the eighth one having twice as many vibrations per second as the first.

OPUS—A musical composition, or group of compositions, usually numbered to indicate the order of its publication within a composer's entire output.

OVERTONES—Faint tones made by the sympathetic vibrations of piano strings other than those that have been struck by hammers.

PEDAL—That part of a piano's mechanism that is controlled by the feet and used to influence tones.

PERCUSSION—Instruments on which the sound is made by striking or shaking. The piano is included in this group.

PIANOLA—A mechanical piano, commonly called a player piano. Pianola was the product of the Aeolian Organ & Music Co. Warren G. Harding, President of the United States, had a pianola in the White House during his administration. The arrival of radio, phonograph, and automobile sent the player piano into temporary oblivion in the late twenties. The instrument was revived in 1961. Six companies now manufacture it, and three outfits make player-piano music rolls, without which this instrument is just another piano. QRS Player Piano Rolls, Inc., of Buffalo, New York, is the oldest music-roll maker, with a catalog of over 2,500 selections.

PIN BLOCK—Of a piano, a long piece of laminated wood—six layers of rock maple—behind the keyboard. It holds tuning pins at the player's end of the piano's frame. Also called a wrest plank.

PITCH—The relative highness or lowness of a musical tone.

PLAYER PIANO—See Pianola.

PLECTRUM—A pick for twanging strings. (The plural is plectra.)

POLYCHORD—A many-stringed instrument evolved from the monochord. See also Monochord.

PREPARED PIANO—One in which small objects are attached to the strings in order to alter their tones.

PRESTISSIMO—A direction for tempo; as fast as instrumentalists are able to play.

PRESTO—Very fast (used as a direction in music).

PSALTERY—A Greek plucked zither of the Middle Ages.

RESONANCE—The reinforcement of sound by the vibration of another body.

RHAPSODY—In Greek, an epic poem; in music, an instrumental composition of heroic or nationalistic character, or one that is elaborate and showy in style.

RHYTHM—The organization of music in respect to time; the regular occurrence of beat.

RIM—Of a piano, the U-shaped wooden edge of the instrument's case.

RONDO—A form of instrumental music in which a recurring theme or section alternates with contrasting themes or sections.

SCALE—A series of tones within an octave which are used as the basis of musical composition.

SONATA—For piano, a composition in three or four movements, usually for one or two instruments.

SONATINA—A sonata with few movements and little development.

SOUND—The sensation of hearing that results from the reaction of the ears' auditory nerves to vibrations carried in air or water.

SOUNDBOARD—Of a piano, a laminated wooden board, which distributes the sounds made by the vibrating strings.

SPINET—A small version of the harpsichord, usually rectangular, but sometimes pentagonal or triangular.

SYMPATHETIC VIBRATION—A vibration of an object independently, in response to tone sounded by a musical instrument of which the object is a part, or by that of another instrument.

SYMPHONY—A rather long orchestral composition, divided into three or four movements, or sections: the first movement is fast; the second movement is slow and lyrical—often in song form, sometimes a theme and variations; the third movement is either a minuet or a scherzo (Italian for "joke"), a fast-paced, whimsical piece of music; the fourth movement, or finale, is either in rondo or theme-and-variations form.

TEMPO—The rate of speed of a musical composition.

THEME—A melodic pattern constituting the basis of a musical composition.

TIMBRE—Quality of musical tone: thin, thick, light, dark, sharp, dull, smooth, rough, warm, cold, etc. Also called tone color.

TONE COLOR—See Timbre.

TOUCH—Of a pianist, the determination and speed with which he strikes the keys.

TUNING PIN—Of a piano, a metal pin inserted in the keyboard

side of the frame. It holds one end of a string and can be turned by a special tool for tuning the string.

VIBRATION—The rapid back-and-forth movement—often invisible—in space of an object against which some force has been applied.

VIRTUOSO—In music, a highly gifted and technically adept concert artist.

VIVACE—Lively (used as a direction in music).

WREST PLANK—See Pin block.

ZITHER—A flat, plucked-string instrument played with the fingers or with plectra.

Suggested Books for Reading and Reference

Pianos and Pianists

APEL, WILLI. *Masters of the Keyboard: A Brief Survey of Pianoforte Music.* Cambridge, Mass.: Harvard University Press, 1947.

BERKOWITZ, FRIEDA PASTOR. *Unfinished Symphony, and Other Stories of Men and Music.* New York: Atheneum Publishers, 1963.

BROCKWAY, WALLACE, AND WEINSTOCK, HERBERT. *Men of Music.* New York: Simon & Schuster, Inc., 1958.

COOKE, CHARLES. *Playing the Piano for Pleasure.* New York: Simon & Schuster, Inc., 1960.

LOESSER, ARTHUR. *Men, Women and Pianos.* New York: Simon & Schuster, Inc., 1954.

NEWMAN, WILLIAM S. *The Pianists' Problems.* New York: Harper & Row, 1956.

SCHONBERG, HAROLD C. *The Great Pianists from Mozart to the Present.* New York: Simon & Schuster, Inc., 1963.

Musical Background

BERNSTEIN, LEONARD. *The Infinite Variety of Music*. New
York: Simon & Schuster, Inc., 1966.

COPLAND, AARON. *Copland on Music*. New York: W. W. Norton & Company, 1963.

MACHLIS, JOSEPH. *Music: Adventures in Listening*. New
York: W. W. Norton & Company, 1968.

MCKINNEY, HOWARD D., AND ANDERSON, W. R. *Discovering
Music*. New York: American Book Company, 1952.

MOORE, DOUGLAS. *Listening to Music*. New York: W. W.
Norton & Company, 1963.

ROEHL, HARVEY. *Player Piano Treasury*. Vestal, N.Y.: Vestal.

SELIGMANN, JEAN, AND DANZIGER, JULIET. *The Meaning of
Music: The Young Concertgoer's Guide*. New York:
World Publishing Company, 1966.

SLONIMSKY, NICOLAS. *The Road to Music*. Dodd, Mead &
Co., 1966.

Reference Books

APEL, WILLI, ed. *Harvard Dictionary of Music*. Second
edition, revised and enlarged. Cambridge, Mass.: Harvard
University Press, 1969.

BAINES, ANTHONY, ed. *Musical Instruments Through the
Ages*. Baltimore: Penguin Books, Inc., 1966.

BAUER, MARION, AND PEYSER, ETHEL. Ed. by E. E. Rogers.
How Music Grew. New York: G. P. Putnam's Sons, 1939.

———. *Music Through the Ages*. New York: G. P. Putnam's
Sons, 1967.

BLOM, ERIC, ed. *Everyman's Dictionary of Music*. New York:
E. P. Dutton & Co., 1962.

DONINGTON, ROBERT. *The Instruments of Music.* New York: Barnes & Noble, 1962.

EINSTEIN, ALFRED. *A Short History of Music.* New York: Alfred A. Knopf, Inc., 1954.

HUGHES, LANGSTON. *The First Book of Jazz.* New York: Franklin Watts, Inc., 1954.

JAMES, PHILIP. *Early Keyboard Instruments.* Chester Springs, Penn.: Dufour Editions, Inc.

SACHS, CURT. *History of Musical Instruments.* New York: W. W. Norton & Company, 1940.

SCHULLER, GUNTHER. *Early Jazz.* New York: Oxford University Press, 1968.

WILLIAMS, MARTIN T. *Jazz Masters of New Orleans.* New York: The Macmillan Company, 1967.

WILLS, VERA G., AND MANNERS, ANDE. *A Parent's Guide to Music Lessons.* New York: Harper & Row, 1967.

A Sampling of Recordings

The following list of recordings is a sampling of the finest of the wide range of piano music available on records. You will find some selections from the basic repertoire, as well as less familiar compositions. Both types of music are rewarding for the attentive listener. The records listed are single LP's, unless otherwise noted. Multi-record sets have been included if they feature performances of special merit or historical importance, or if they contain desirable performances that are unavailable on a single LP. The listings are drawn from the Schwann Catalog, the standard guide to Long Playing records, which is issued monthly.

Many schools have facilities for listening to records, and a growing number of libraries have records available for loan. If you hear a performance that you'd like to own, investigate whether it is available on an inexpensive recording. Some of the leading record companies have budget labels that feature excellent performances and good sound at low prices. Whenever possible these inexpensive labels have been included in this discography.

Classical

BACH, JOHANN SEBASTIAN (1685–1750)
  Bach Program; Biggs (harpsichord). Columbia MS-6804.
  Goldberg Variations; Gould (piano). Columbia MS-7096.
  Sonatas for Flute and Harpsichord; Wummer, Valenti.
    Westminster 49084 (4-record set).
  Well-Tempered Clavier; Landowska (harpsichord). RCA
    Victor LM-6801 (6-record set).
BACH, CARL PHILIPP EMANUEL (1714–1788)
  Sonatas for Piano; Katzenellenbogen. Lyrichord 63.
BARBER, SAMUEL (1910–   )
  Sonata, opus 26; Horowitz. RCA Victor LD-7021 (2-
    record set).
BARTÓK, BÉLA (1881–1945)
  Concerto No. 1 for Piano and Orchestra; Peter Serkin, with
    Chicago Symphony under Ozawa. RCA Victor LSC-
    2929.
  Concerto No. 2 for Piano and Orchestra; Entremont, with
    New York Philharmonic under Bernstein. Columbia
    MS-7145.
  Concerto No. 3 for Piano and Orchestra; Peter Serkin, with
    Chicago Symphony under Ozawa. RCA Victor LSC-
    2929. (Coupled with Bartók Concerto No. 1.)
  Mikrokosmos (excerpts); Bartók. Odyssey 32160220.
  Mikrokosmos (complete); Sándor. Vox SVBX-5425 (3-
    record set).
  Rhapsody for Piano, opus 1; Hambro. Bartók 313.
BEETHOVEN, LUDWIG VAN (1770–1827)
  Concerto No. 1 in C for Piano and Orchestra, opus 15;
    Rubinstein, with Boston Symphony under Leinsdorf.
    RCA Victor LSC-3013.
  Concerto No. 4 in G for Piano and Orchestra, opus 58;

Cliburn with Chicago Symphony under Reiner. RCA Victor LSC-2680.

Fantasia in C Minor for Piano, Chorus, and Orchestra, opus 80; Rudolf Serkin, with New York Philharmonic under Bernstein, and Westminster Chorus. Columbia MS-6616.

Quintet in E-flat for Piano and Winds, opus 16; Ashkenazy, with London Wind Soloists. London 6494.

Sonata No. 1 in F Minor for Piano, opus 2, No. 1; Backhaus. London 6389.

Sonata No. 3 in C for Piano, opus 2, No. 3; Hofmann. Archive of Piano Music X903.

Sonata No. 8 in C Minor, opus 13, "Pathetique"; R. Serkin. Columbia MS-6481.

Sonata No. 14 in C-sharp Minor for Piano, opus 27, No. 2, "Moonlight"; Paderewski. Archive of Piano Music X926.

Sonata No. 15 in D for Piano, opus 28, "Pastoral"; Backhaus. London 6247.

Sonata No. 21 in C, opus 53, "Waldstein"; Gieseking. Odyssey 32160314.

Sonata No. 23 in F Minor for Piano, opus 57, "Appassionata"; Horowitz. RCA Victor LSC-2366.

Sonata No. 26 in E-flat for Piano, opus 81a, "Les Adieux," and *Sonata No. 27 in E Minor,* opus 90; Backhaus. London 6247.

5 Sonatas for Cello and Piano (complete) ; Casals (cello), Rudolf Serkin (piano). Odyssey 32360016 (3-record set) .

BRAHMS, JOHANNES (1833–97)

Concerto No. 1 in D Minor for Piano and Orchestra, opus 15; Cliburn, with Boston Symphony under Leinsdorf. RCA Victor LSC-2724.

Concerto No. 2 in B-flat for Piano and Orchestra, opus 83;

Gilels, with Chicago Symphony under Reiner. RCA Victor LSC-2581. . . . Horowitz, with NBC Symphony under Toscanini. RCA Victor LCT-1025.

Piano Music from opuses 76, 79, 117/19; Rubinstein. RCA Victor LM-1787.

Piano Pieces from opuses 79, 118, 119; Gieseking. Angel 35027.

Quintet in F Minor for Piano and Strings, opus 34; Eschenbach, with Amadeus Quartet. Deutsche Grammophon Gesellschaft (DGG) 139397.

Trio in A Minor for Clarinet, Cello, and Piano, opus 114; Geuser, Troester, Hansen (Beethoven Trio). Mace S-9038.

Trio in E-flat for Horn, Violin, and Piano, opus 40; Bloom, Tree, and Rudolf Serkin. Columbia MS-7266.

CAGE, JOHN (1912–)

Amores for Prepared Piano and Percussion; Manhattan Percussion Ensemble. Mainstream 5011.

Concerto for Prepared Piano and Chamber Orchestra; Takahashi, with Buffalo Philharmonic under Foss. Nonesuch 71202.

Indeterminacy; Cage (narrator), Tudor (piano). Folkways 3704 (2-record set).

Sonatas and Interludes for Prepared Piano; Ajemian. Composers Recordings, Inc. 199.

CASADESUS, ROBERT (1899–)

Pièces Pour Deux Pianos (6); J. and D. Lang. Golden Crest S-4070.

CHOPIN, FRÉDÉRIC (1810–49)

Concerto No. 1 in E Minor for Piano and Orchestra, opus 11; Graffman, with Boston Symphony under Munch. RCA Victor VICS-1030.

Concerto No. 2 in F Minor with Piano and Orchestra, opus

21; Ashkenazy, with London Symphony under Zinman. London 6440.

Études (opus 10); Arrau. Angel 35143.

Mazurkas (51); Brailowsky. Columbia MS-6402, 6464/5 (3-record set).

Nocturnes (4); de Pachmann. Archive of Piano Music X-921.

Piano Music; Godowsky. Veritas 103.

Polonaises; Rubinstein. RCA Victor LM-1205.

Preludes (Nos. 1, 3, 7, 23); Busoni. Archive of Piano Music X-906.

Preludes, opus 28; Rubinstein. RCA Victor LM-1163.

CLEMENTI, MUZIO (1752–1832)

Sonatas (opuses 14, 26/2, 34); Horowitz. RCA Victor LM-1902.

COPLAND, AARON (1900–　)

Concerto for Piano and Orchestra (1927); Copland, with New York Philharmonic under Bernstein. Columbia MS-6698.

Passacaglia for Piano; Aitken. Lyrichord 104.

Piano Fantasy; Masselos. Odyssey 32160040.

Sonata for Piano; Aitken. Lyrichord 104.

COWELL, HENRY (1897–1965)

Piano Music; Cowell, Folkways 3349.

Sonata No. 1 for Violin and Piano; Szigeti, Bussotti. Columbia CML-4841.

Toccanta for Soprano, Flute, Cello, and Piano; Boatwright, Ensemble. Columbia CML-4986.

DEBUSSY, CLAUDE (1862–1918)

Children's Corner Suite; Gieseking. Angel 35067.

Claire de Lune, from Suite Bergamasque; Iturbi. RCA Victor LM-1967.

Preludes, Book 1; Gieseking. Angel 35066.

FIELD, JOHN (1782–1837)

Concerto No. 2 for Piano and Orchestra; Kyriakou, with Berlin Symphony under Bünte. Candide 31006.

Nocturnes (7); Kyriakou. Candide 31006; coupled with John Field Concerto No. 2 (above).

GERSHWIN, GEORGE (1898–1937)

Concerto in F; Nero, with Boston Pops Orchestra under Fiedler. RCA Victor LSC-3025.

"I Got Rhythm," Variations for Piano and Orchestra; Pennario, with Hollywood Bowl Symphony under Newman. Capitol SP-8581.

Music of Gershwin; George Gershwin (piano). Movietone 71009.

Rhapsody in Blue; Pennario, with Paul Whiteman Orchestra. Capitol SP-8675. . . . List, with Eastman-Rochester Orchestra, under Hanson. Mercury 9002. . . . Wild, with Boston Pops Orchestra under Fiedler. RCA Victor LSC-2746.

GRIEG, EDVARD (1843–1907)

Concerto in A Minor for Piano; Lipatti, with Philharmonia Orchestra under Galliera. Odyssey 32160141. (Coupled with Schumann: Concerto in A Minor for Piano and Orchestra; see entry under SCHUMANN, ROBERT.)

Norwegian Dances, opus 35; W. Klien, B. Klien. Turnabout 34041.

HARRIS, ROY (1898–   )

Quintet for Piano and Strings (1936); J. Harris, with American Art Quartet. Contemporary 8012.

Trio (piano) (1934); University of Oklahoma Trio. University of Oklahoma 1.

HAYDN, FRANZ JOSEPH (1732–1809)

Sonatas for Piano (Nos. 34, 48, 52); Backhaus. London STS-15041.

Concerto in D for Harpsichord, opus 21; Landowska. Seraphim 60116.

IVES, CHARLES (1874–1954)

Piano Music (complete); Mandel. Desto 6458/61 (4-record set).

Sonata No. 1 for Piano; Masselos. Odyssey 32160059.

Sonata No. 2 (Concord, Mass., 1840–1860); Pappastavrou (piano), Lichter (flute). Composers Recordings, Inc. 150. . . . Mandel. Desto 6458/61 (see Piano Music, complete, above).

LISZT, FRANZ (1811–86)

Concerto No. 1 in E-flat for Piano and Orchestra; Watts, with New York Philharmonic under Bernstein. Columbia MS-6955.

Concerto Pathétique for Piano; Vronsky, Babin. Decca 9790.

Hungarian Rhapsodies for Piano; Brendel. Vanguard C-10035.

Mephisto Waltz; Rubinstein. RCA Victor LM 1905.

Reminiscences of Don Juan (after Mozart); Ogdon. Seraphim S-60088.

Wanderer Fantasy for Piano and Orchestra (after Schubert); Brendel, with Vienna Volksoper Orchestra under Gielen. Turnabout 324650.

Weihnachtsbaum (Christmas Tree) (12 Pieces for Piano); Kabos. Bartok 910.

MACDOWELL, EDWARD (1861–1908)

Concerto No. 2 in D Minor for Piano and Orchestra, opus 23; Cliburn, with Chicago Symphony under Hendl. RCA Victor LSC-2507.

Woodland Sketches, opus 51; Rivkin. Westminster 9310.

MENDELSSOHN, FELIX (1809–47)

Capriccio Brillant for Piano and Orchestra, opus 22; Graffman, with Boston Symphony under Munch. RCA Victor VICS-1030.

Concerto No. 1 in G Minor for Piano and Orchestra, opus 25; R. Serkin, with Philadelphia Orchestra under Ormandy. Columbia MS-7185. (Coupled with Mendelssohn: *Concerto No. 2 in D Minor for Piano and Orchestra,* with the same artists.)

Concerto in E for 2 Pianos and Orchestra; Gold, Fizdale, with Philadelphia Orchestra under Ormandy. Columbia MS-6681.

Rondo Capriccioso in E, opus 14; Hofmann. Superscope 4100A003.

Songs Without Words; Novaes. Turnabout 34245.

MENOTTI, GIAN CARLO (1911–)

Concerto in F; Wild, with Symphony of the Air under Mester. Vanguard 2094.

MOZART, WOLFGANG AMADEUS (1756–91)

Concerto No. 9 in E-flat for Piano and Orchestra, K.271; Serkin, with Marlboro Festival Orchestra under Schneider. Columbia CML-5209.

Concerto No. 20 in D Minor for Piano and Orchestra, K.466; Haskil, with Vienna Symphony under Paumgartner. Mercury 90413.

Concerto No. 23 in A for Piano and Orchestra, K.488; Curzon, with London Symphony Orchestra under Kertész. London 6580.

Piano Music for Four Hands (complete); Haebler, Hoffman, Brendel, Klien, Angerer. Vox SVBX-566 (3-record set).

Quintet in E-flat for Piano and Winds, K.452; Ashkenazy, with London Wind Soloists. London 6494.

Sonata No. 8 in A Minor, K.310; Kempff. Deutsche Gram-

mophon Gesellschaft (DGG) 138707. . . . Lipatti.
Odyssey 32160320.

MUSSORGSKY, MODEST (1839–81)

Pictures at an Exhibition; Vladimir Horowitz. RCA Victor
LM-2357.

PADEREWSKI, IGNACE JAN (1860–1941)

Piano Music; Paderewski. Archive of Piano Music X-901.

PROKOFIEV, SERGEI (1891–1953)

Concerto No. 1 in D-flat for Piano and Orchestra, opus 10;
Graffman, with Cleveland Orchestra under Szell. Columbia MS-6925.

Concerto No. 3 in C for Piano and Orchestra, opus 26;
Petrov, with Moscow Radio Symphony under Rozhdest-
vensky. Melodiya-Angel S-40042.

Piano Music; Prokofiev. Archive of Piano Music X-907.

RACHMANINOFF, SERGEI (1873–1943)

Concerto No. 2 in C Minor for Piano and Orchestra, opus
18; Richter, with Warsaw Philharmonic under Wislocki.
Deutsche Grammophon Gesellschaft (DGG) 138076.

Miscellaneous Piano Pieces; Rachmaninoff. RCA Victor
LM-2587.

*Rhapsody for Piano and Orchestra on a Theme by Paga-
nini,* opus 43; Katchen, with London Symphony under
Boult. London 6153.

RAVEL, MAURICE (1875–1937)

Concerto in D for the Left Hand; Casadesus, with Philadelphia Orchestra under Ormandy, Columbia 6274.

Ma Mère l'Oye (Mother Goose, Four-Hand Piano Suite);
W. Klien, B. Klien. Turnabout 34235.

Piano Music (complete); Casadesus, Odyssey 32360003
(3-record set).

SAINT-SAËNS, CAMILLE (1835–1921)

Carnival of the Animals; Beatrice Lillie (narrator), Katchen,

Graffman, with London Symphony Orchestra under Henderson. London 6187.

Concerto No. 2 in G Minor for Piano and Orchestra, opus 22; Gilels, with Paris Conservatory Orchestra under Cluytens. Angel 35132.

SCHÖNBERG, ARNOLD (1874–1951)

Concerto for Piano and Orchestra, opus 42; Brendel, with SW German Radio Symphony under Gielen. Turnabout 34051.

SCHUBERT, FRANZ (1797–1828)

Four-Hand Piano Pieces; Badura-Skoda, Demus. Westminster 9353/4 (2-record set) .

Impromptus; Brendel. Vox 512390.

Moments Musicaux, opus 94; Gilels. Melodiya-Angel S-40082.

Quintet in A, "Trout," opus 11; P. Serkin, Schneider, Tree, Soyer, Levine. Vanguard 71145.

Sonata for Piano, Violin, Cello (Trio in B-flat) ; Y. and H. Menuhin, Gendron. Angel S-36614.

Sonata in A for Piano, opus 120; Ashkenazy. London 6500.

SCHUMANN, ROBERT (1810–56)

Arabeske, opus 18; Horowitz. Seraphim 60114.

Carnaval, opus 9; Novaes. Turnabout 34164.

Concerto in A Minor for Piano and Orchestra, opus 54; Lipatti, with Philharmonia Orchestra under Karajan. Odyssey 32160141. (Coupled with Grieg: *Concerto in A Minor for Piano;* see entry under GRIEG, EDVARD.)

SHOSTAKOVICH, DMITRI (1906–)

Concerto No. 2 for Piano and Orchestra, opus 101 (1957) ; Bernstein, with New York Philharmonic Orchestra. Columbia MS-6043.

Preludes and Fugues (24) , opus 87 (1951) ; Shostakovich. Seraphim 60024.

STRAVINSKY, IGOR (1882–   )
   Petrouchka: 3 Scenes; Y. Menuhin, J. Ryce. Everest 3130.
   Sonata for 2 Pianos; 3 Easy Pieces; 5 Easy Pieces; Gold, Fizdale. Columbia CMS-6333.
TCHAIKOVSKY, PETER ILYITCH (1840–93)
   Concerto No. 1 in B-flat Minor for Piano and Orchestra, opus 23; Horowitz, with NBC Symphony under Toscanini. RCA Victor LM-2319.
   Piano Music; Entremont. Columbia MS-6446.
TCHEREPNIN, ALEXANDER (1899–   )
   Bagatelles, opus 5; Weber, with Berlin Radio Symphony under Fricsay. Deutsche Grammophon Gesellschaft (DGG) 138710.
   Trio for Piano and Strings, opus 34; Pro Musica Trio. Pro Musica 201.
WEBER, CARL MARIA VON (1786–1826)
   Konzertstück in F Minor, opus 79; Arrau, Philharmonia Orchestra under Galliera. Seraphim S-60020.

Jazz (Listed by performers)

BASIE, WILLIAM "COUNT"
   Count Basie in Kansas City. RCA Victor LPV-514.
BRUBECK, DAVE
   At Carnegie Hall. Columbia C2S-826 (2-record set).
   Impressions of Eurasia. Columbia CS-8058.
   Impressions of Japan. Columbia CS-9012.
   Solo Piano (1957). Fantasy 3259.
CHARLES, RAY
   Live Concert. ABC S-500.
   Man and His Soul. ABC S-590X (2-record set).
   Recipe for Soul. ABC S-465.

ELLINGTON, EDWARD "DUKE"
  Afro-Bossa. Reprise 96069.
  The Ellington Era, Vol. 1. Columbia C3L-27 (3-record set).
  Nutcracker, Peer Gynt. Odyssey 32160252.
EVANS, BILL
  At Shelly's Manne Hole. Riverside S-3013.
  Live at Montreux. Verve 168762.
GARNER, ERROLL
  Garner, Vols. 1 & 2. Savoy 12002/3 (2-record set).
  Greatest Garner. Atlantic 1227.
  One More Time. Harmony 11268.
  Up in Erroll's Room. MGM S-4520.
HANCOCK, HERBIE
  Speak Like a Child. Blue Note 84279.
HINES, EARL "FATHA"
  Blows Best. Decca 75048.
  Real, in Concert. Focus S-335.
  Southside Swing. Decca 79221.
JAMAL, AHMAD
  Bright, Blue and Beautiful. Cadet S-807.
  Chamber Music of New Jazz. Cadet 602.
  Roar of Greasepaint. Cadet S-751.
JOHNSON, JAMES P.
  New York Jazz. Stinson 21.
  Yamekraw. Folkways-Scholastic 2842.
JONES, HANK
  Have You Met Hank Jones. Savoy 12084.
LEWIS, MEADE LUX
  Meade Lux Lewis. Stinson 25.
LEWIS, RAMSEY
  Bach to the Blues. Cadet S-732.
  Bossa Nova. Cadet S-705.

You Better Believe Me. Cadet S-750.

MENDES, SERGIO

Best of Brazil. Atlantic S-1480.

In the Brazilian Bag. Tower ST-5052.

Swinger from Rio. Atlantic S-1434.

MONK, THELONIOUS

Misterioso. Columbia CS-9216.

Monk's Blues. Columbia CS-9806.

Plays Duke. Riverside S-3015.

Two Hours. Riverside S-3020X (2-record set).

Underground. Columbia CS-9632.

MORTON, JELLY ROLL

Great. Orpheum 103.

Hot Jazz. Victor LPV-524.

I Thought I Heard. Victor LPV-559.

Immortal. Milestone 2003.

Mr. Jelly Lord. Victor LPV-546.

Stomps and Joys. Victor LPV-508.

PETERSON, OSCAR

At Concertgebouw. Verve 68268.

Plays Count Basie. Verve 68092.

TATUM, ART

Legendary. Movietone 72021.

Piano Starts Here. Columbia CS-9655.

WALLER, THOMAS "FATS"

Fats Waller Piano Solo, Ain't Misbehavin'. RCA Victor
    LPM-1246.

Fractious Fingering. RCA Victor LPV-537.

Recordings for Historical Reference

Famous Pianists at the Turn of the Century. Telefunken 37.
The Golden Age of Virtuosi. Argo DA-42/3.
Musicians of the Past. Audio Masterworks 1203.
The Story of Jazz (Langston Hughes). Folkways Jazz Series,
    vols. 1–11. Folkways-Scholastic 2801–2811. (Volume 3 in-
    cludes Morton's "Mournful Serenade.")

Virtuoso Performance Recordings

Harold Bauer Concert. Archive of Piano Music X-911.
Godowsky Recital. Veritas 103.
Hambro and Zayde. Command S-11023.
Horowitz at Carnegie Hall. Columbia M2S-728 (2-record
    set).
Dinu Lipatti—Last Recital. Angel 3556 (2-record set).
Six Legendary Pianists: Cortot, Fischer, Gieseking, Hess,
    Schnabel, Solomon. Seraphim 6045 (3-record set).
The Unforgettable William Kapell. RCA Victor LM-2588.

Index